Magic Boy &
the Robot Elf © 2003
by James Kochalka.
Published by Top Shelf
Productions, PO Box 1282,
Marietta, GA 30061-1282.
www.topshelfcomix.com
Top Shelf Productions and the
Top Shelf logo are © and ™ 2003 by
Top Shelf Productions, Inc.

Kochalka, James
Magic Boy & the Robot Elf/James Kochalka
ISBN: 1-891830-33-3
1. Graphic Novels
2. Science Fiction
3. Cartoons

First Printing, printed in Canada

Magic Boy & the Robot Elf
by James Kochalka

TOP SHELF PRODUCTIONS
MARIETTA, GA

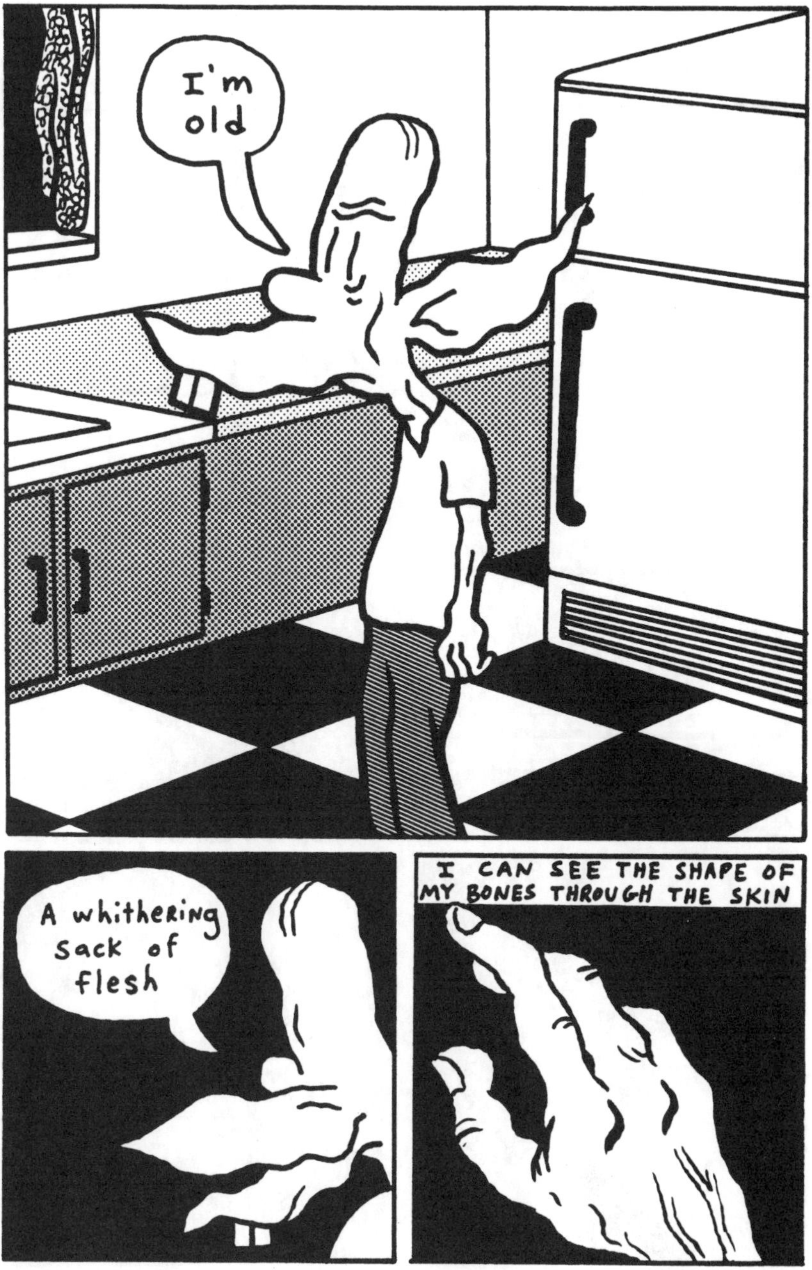
I'm old
A whithering sack of flesh
I CAN SEE THE SHAPE OF MY BONES THROUGH THE SKIN

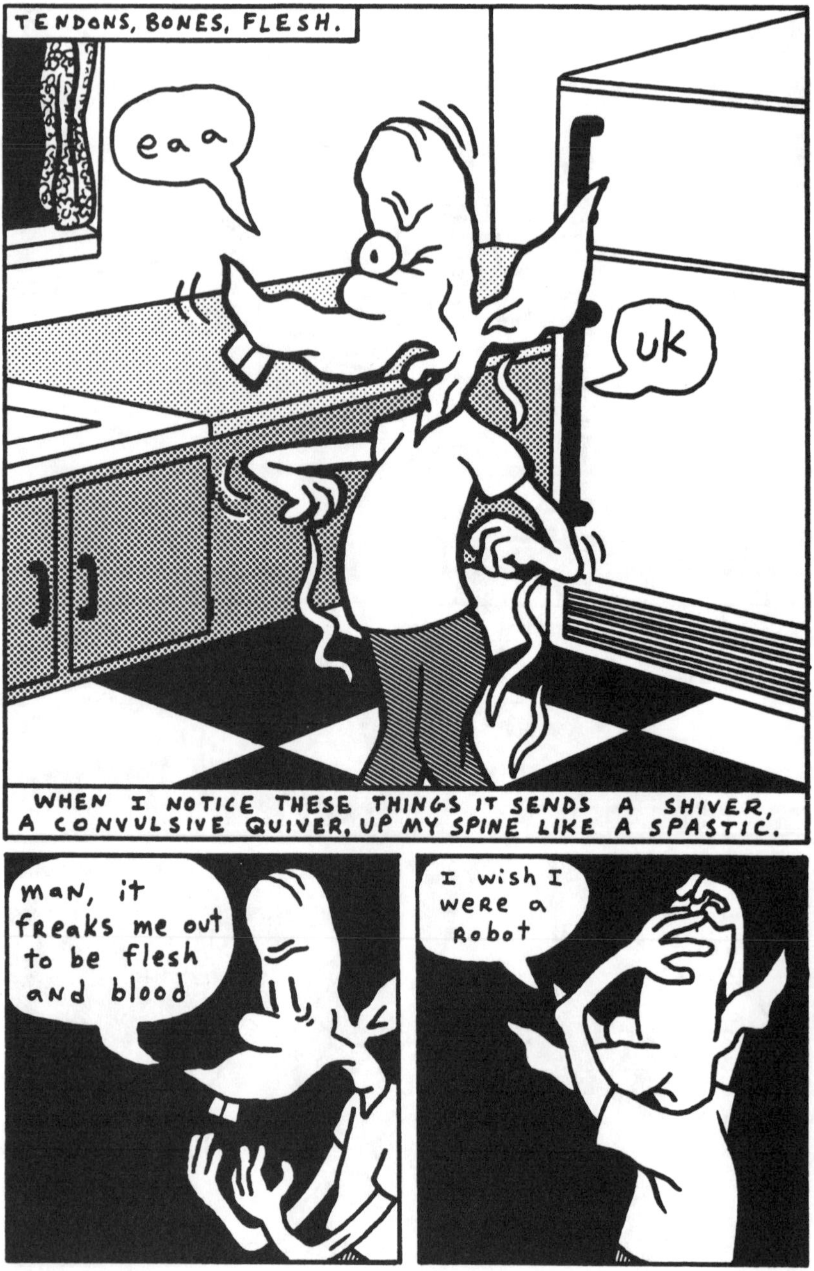
TENDONS, BONES, FLESH.
eaa
uk
WHEN I NOTICE THESE THINGS IT SENDS A SHIVER, A CONVULSIVE QUIVER, UP MY SPINE LIKE A SPASTIC.
man, it freaks me out to be flesh and blood
I wish I were a Robot

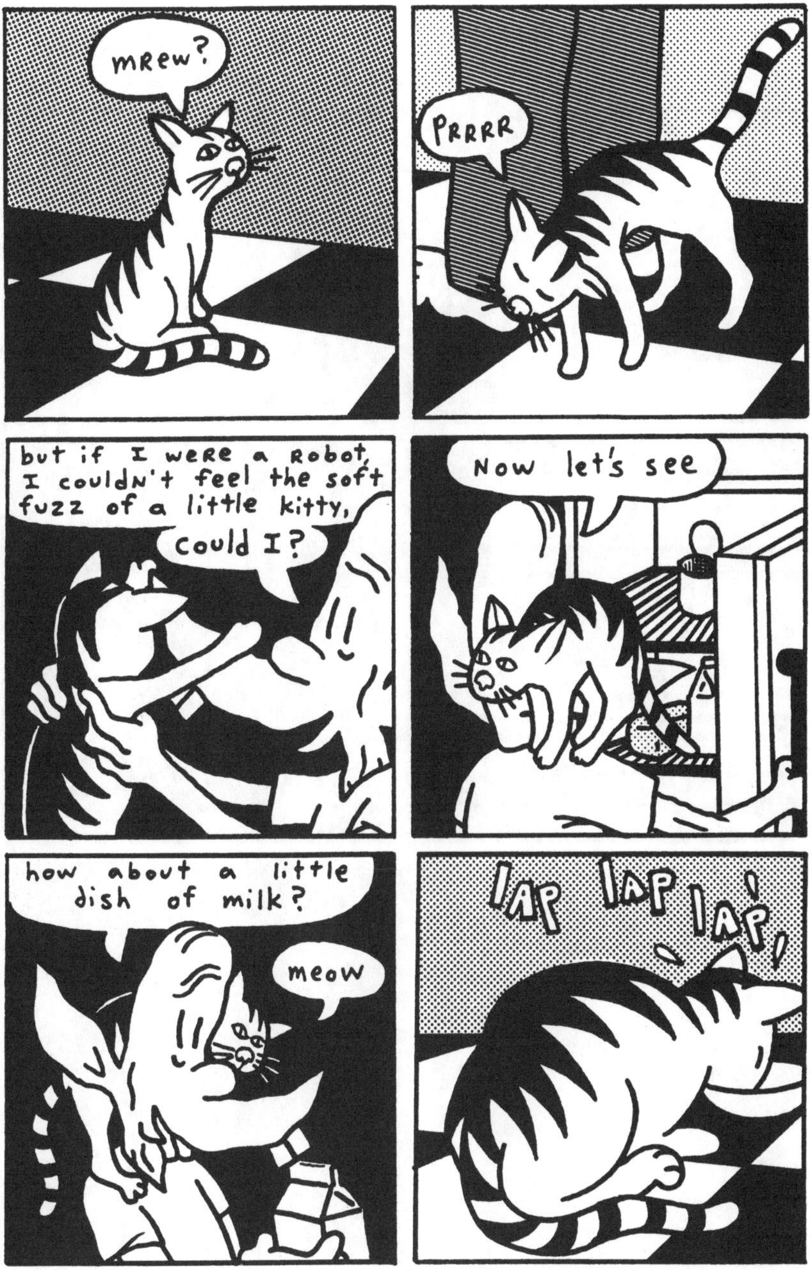
mrew?
PRRRR
but if I were a robot, I couldn't feel the soft fuzz of a little kitty,
could I?
Now let's see
how about a little dish of milk?
meow
lap lap lap

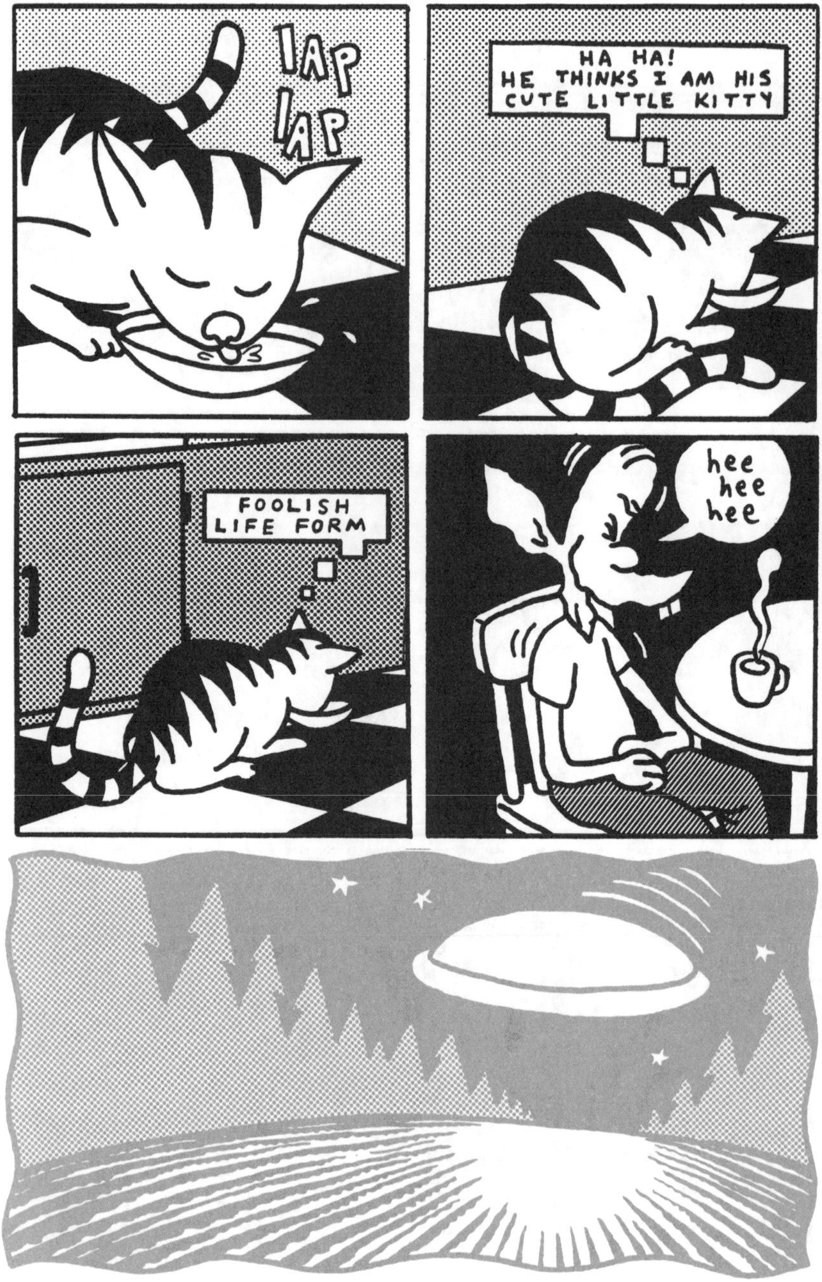
LAP LAP
HA HA!
HE THINKS I AM HIS CUTE LITTLE KITTY
FOOLISH LIFE FORM
hee hee hee

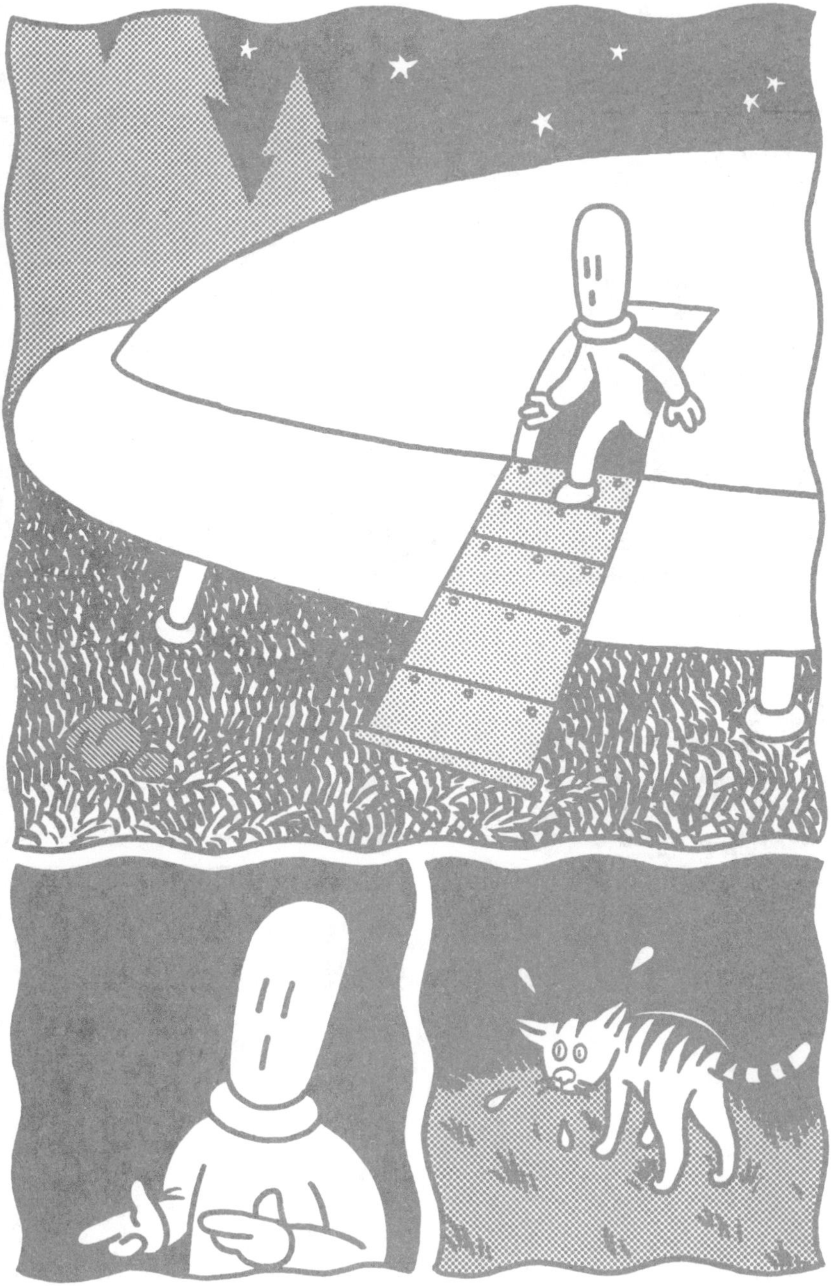

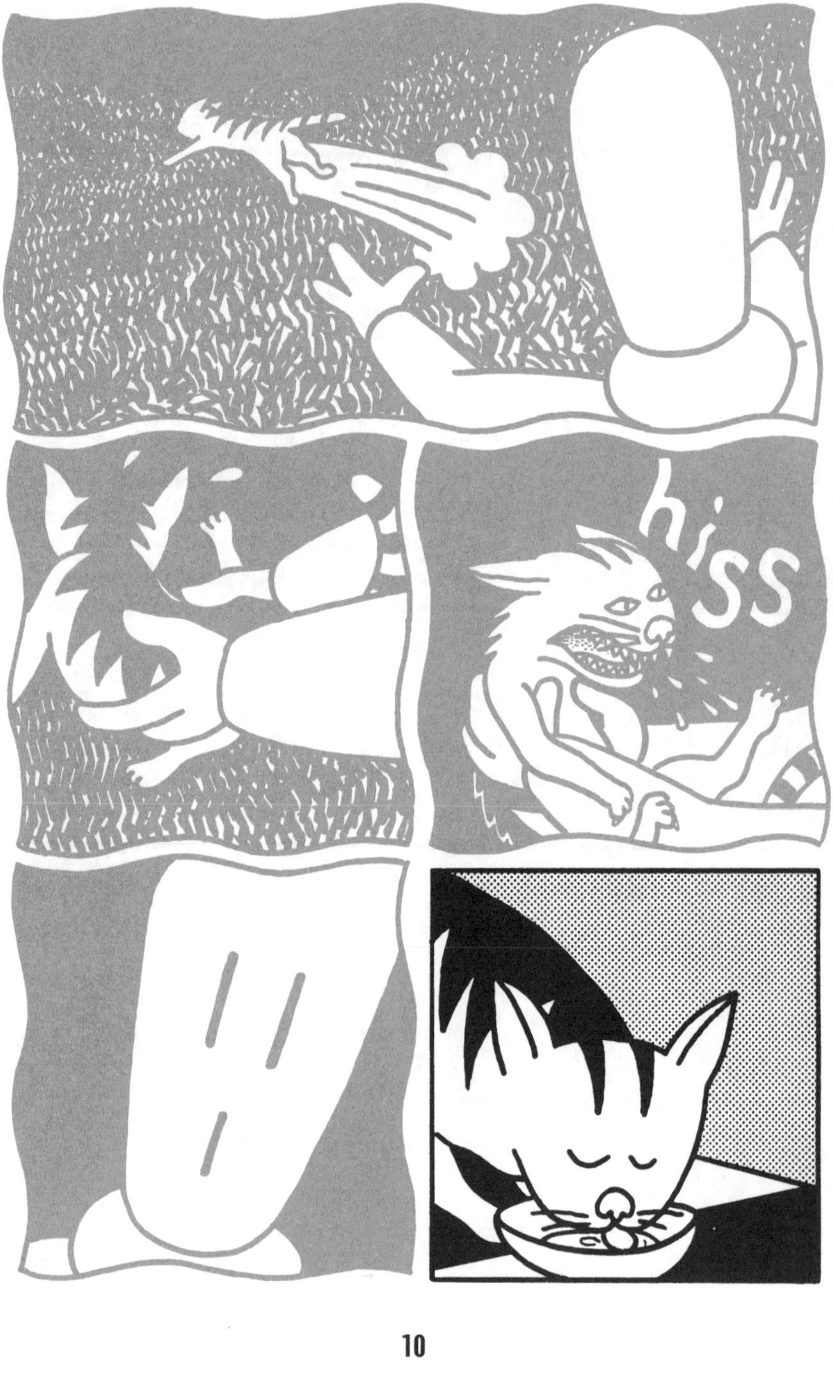
hiss

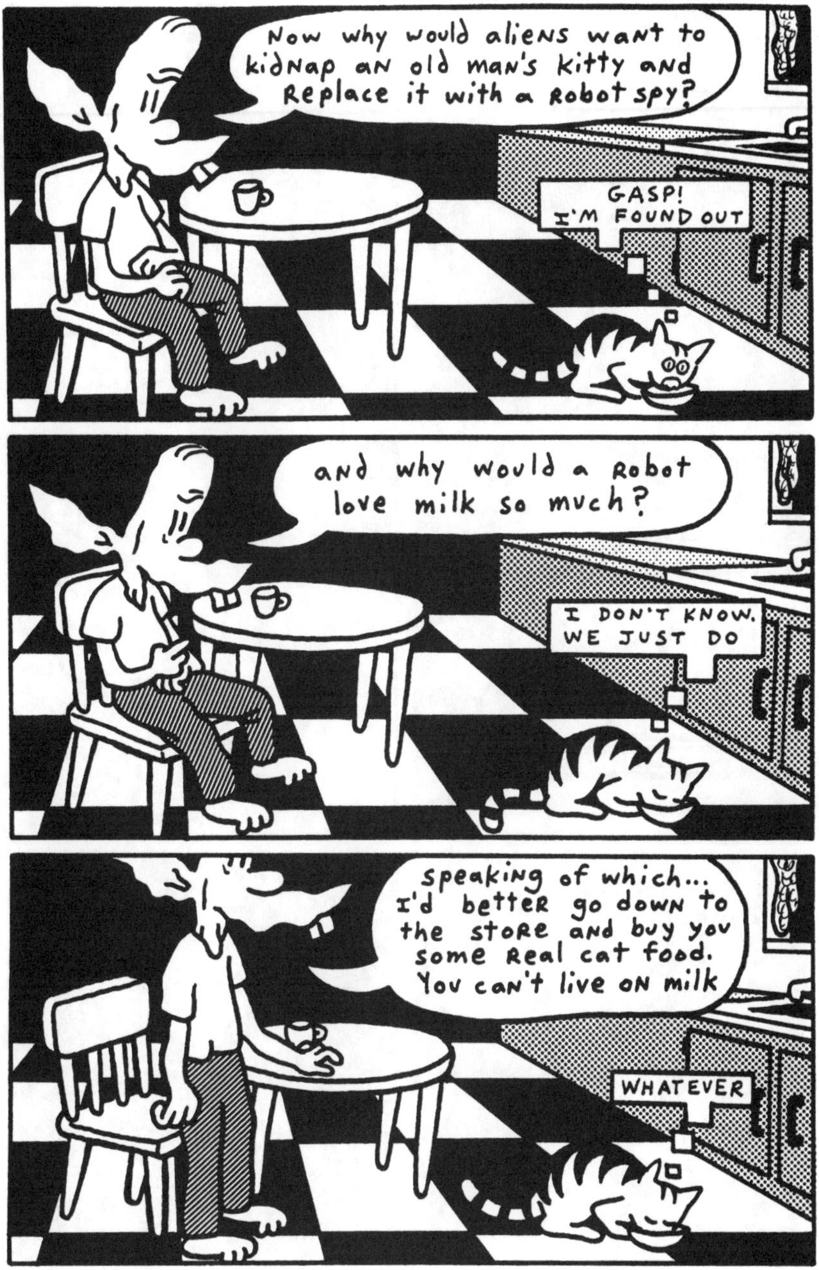
Now why would aliens want to kidnap an old man's kitty and replace it with a robot spy?
GASP! I'M FOUND OUT
and why would a robot love milk so much?
I DON'T KNOW. WE JUST DO
speaking of which... I'd better go down to the store and buy you some real cat food. You can't live on milk
WHATEVER

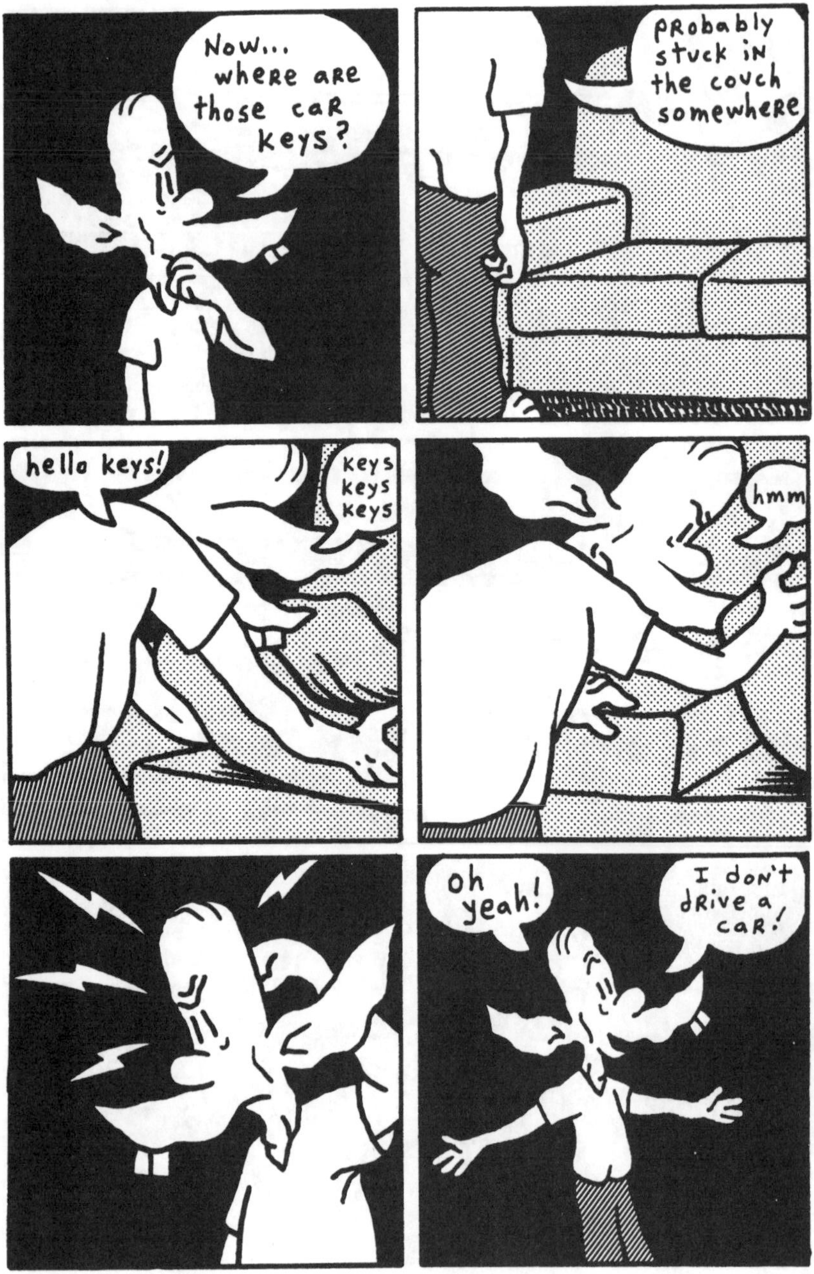
Now... where are those car keys?
probably stuck in the couch somewhere
hello keys!
keys keys keys
hmm
oh yeah!
I don't drive a car!

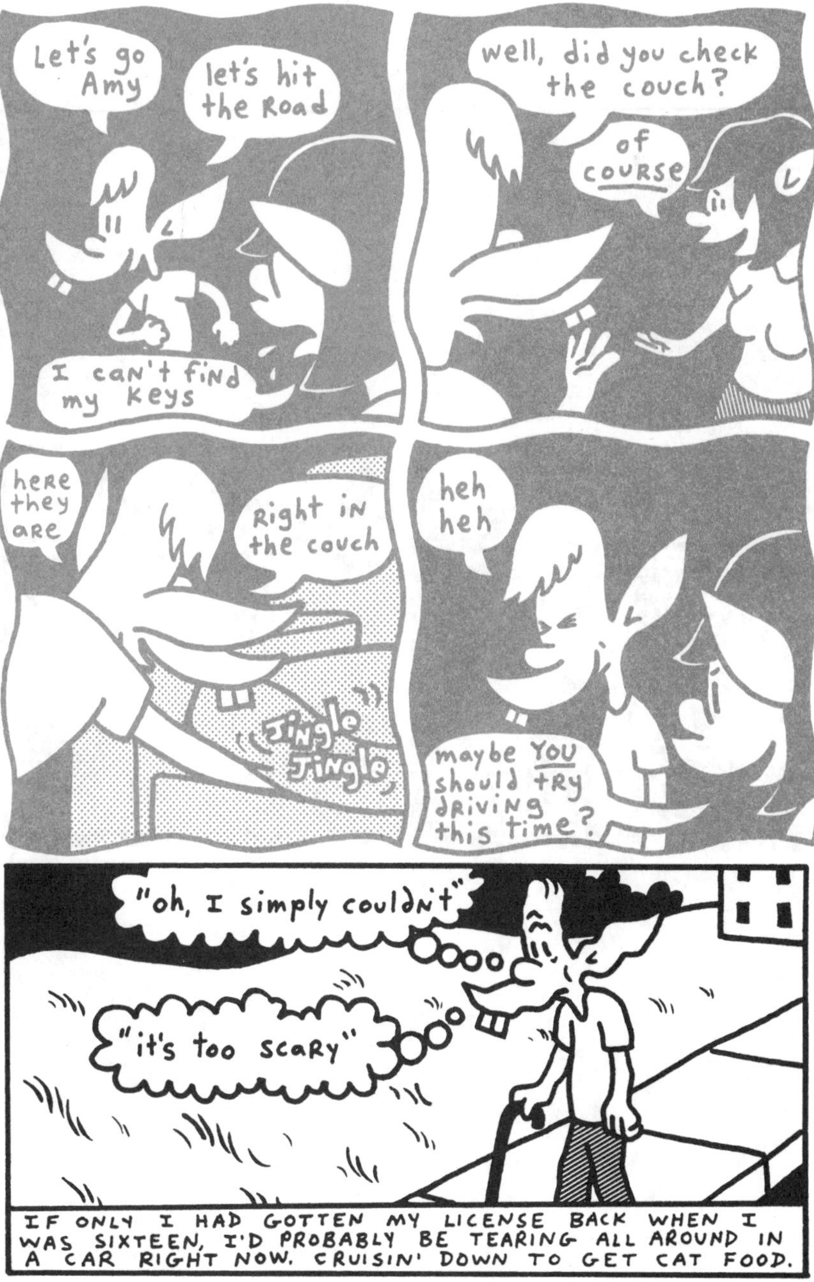
Let's go Amy
let's hit the Road
I can't find my keys
well, did you check the couch?
of COURSE
here they are
Right in the couch
Jingle Jingle
heh heh
maybe YOU should try driving this time?
"oh, I simply couldn't"
"it's too scary"
IF ONLY I HAD GOTTEN MY LICENSE BACK WHEN I WAS SIXTEEN, I'D PROBABLY BE TEARING ALL AROUND IN A CAR RIGHT NOW. CRUISIN' DOWN TO GET CAT FOOD.

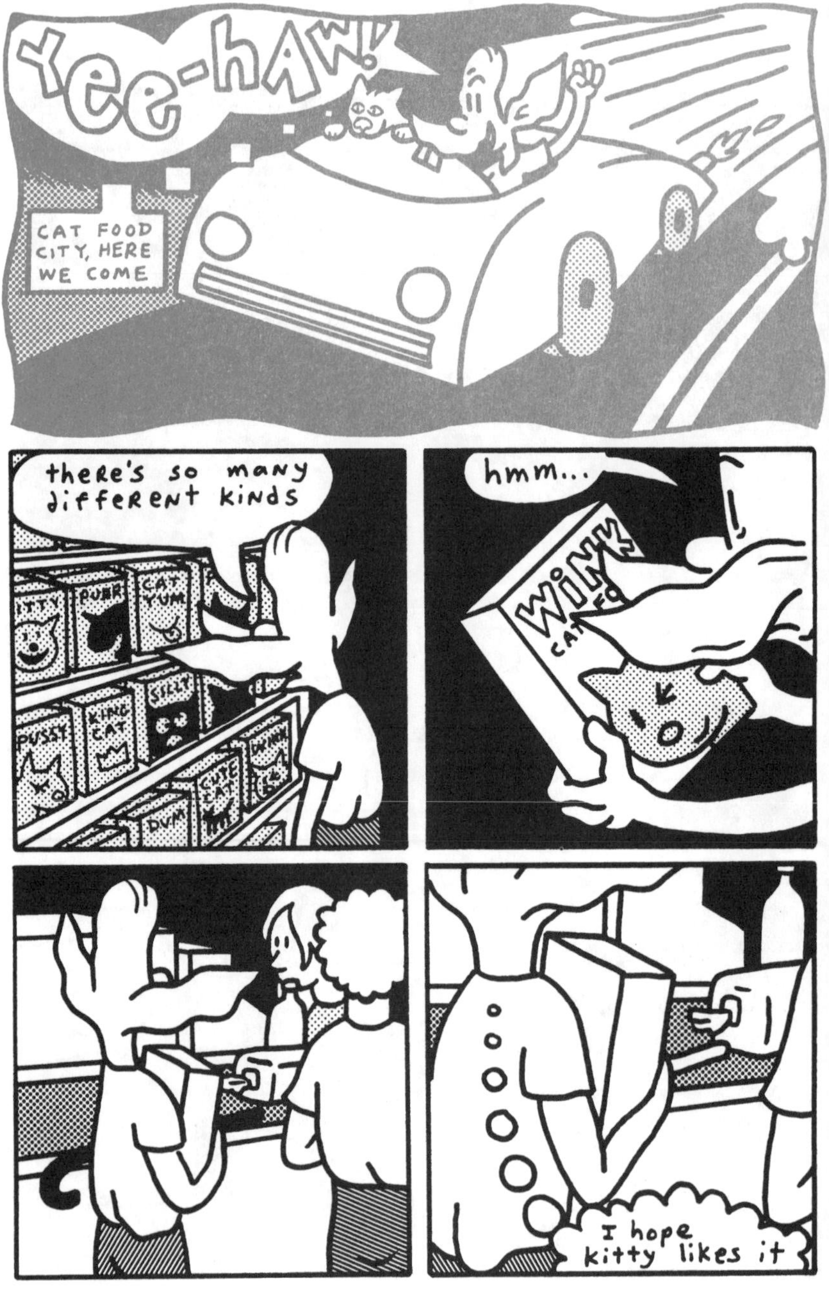
YEE-HAW!
CAT FOOD CITY, HERE WE COME
there's so many different kinds
PURR
CAT YUM
SILLY
PUSSY
KING CAT
CUTE CAT
DUM
hmm...
WINK
I hope kitty likes it

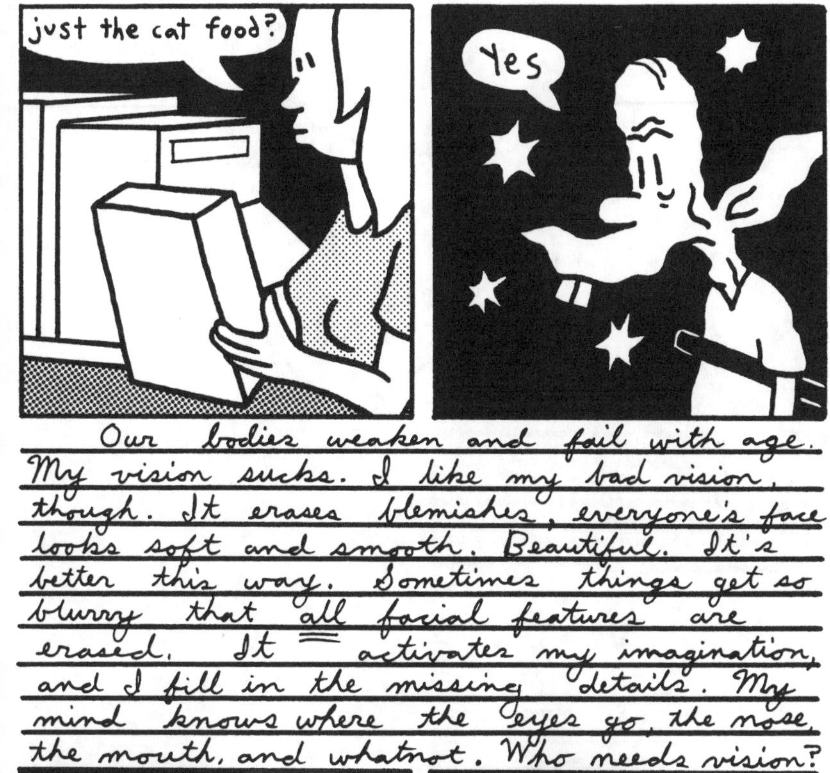
just the cat food?
Yes

Our bodies weaken and fail with age. My vision sucks. I like my bad vision, though. It erases blemishes, everyone's face looks soft and smooth. Beautiful. It's better this way. Sometimes things get so blurry that all facial features are erased. It activates my imagination, and I fill in the missing details. My mind knows where the eyes go, the nose, the mouth, and whatnot. Who needs vision?

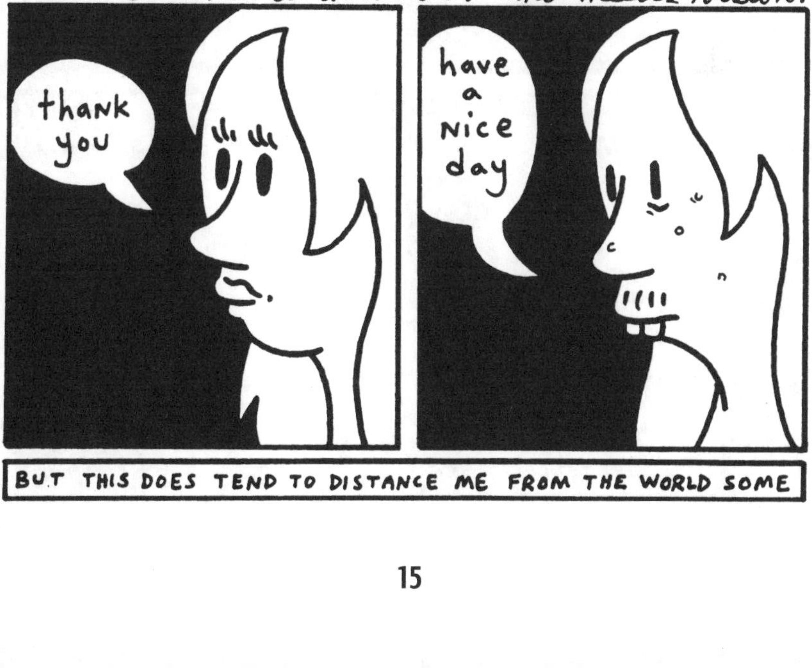
thank you
have a nice day
BUT THIS DOES TEND TO DISTANCE ME FROM THE WORLD SOME

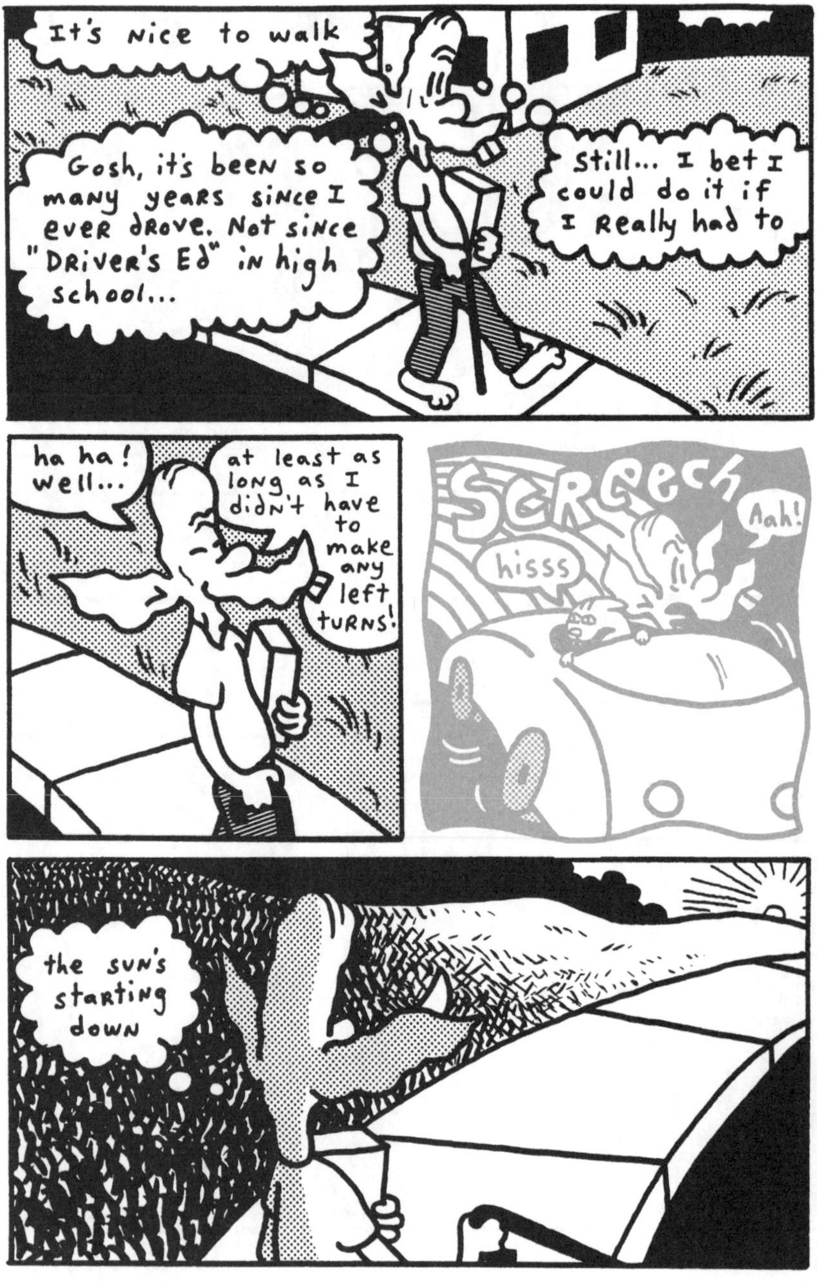
It's nice to walk
Gosh, it's been so many years since I ever drove. Not since "Driver's Ed" in high school...
Still... I bet I could do it if I really had to
ha ha! well...
at least as long as I didn't have to make any left turns!
SCREECH
hisss
Aah!
the sun's starting down

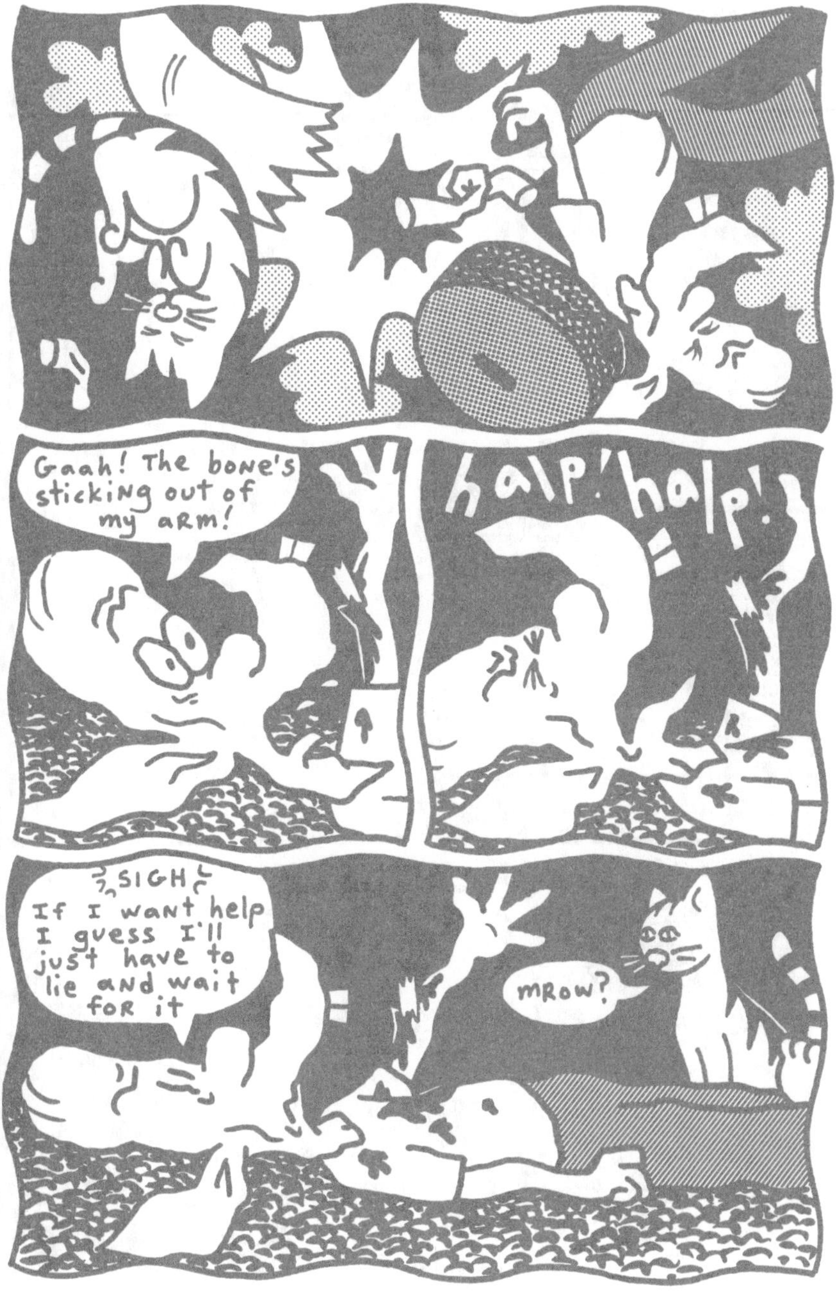
Gaah! The bone's sticking out of my arm!
halp! halp!
SIGH
If I want help I guess I'll just have to lie and wait for it
mRow?

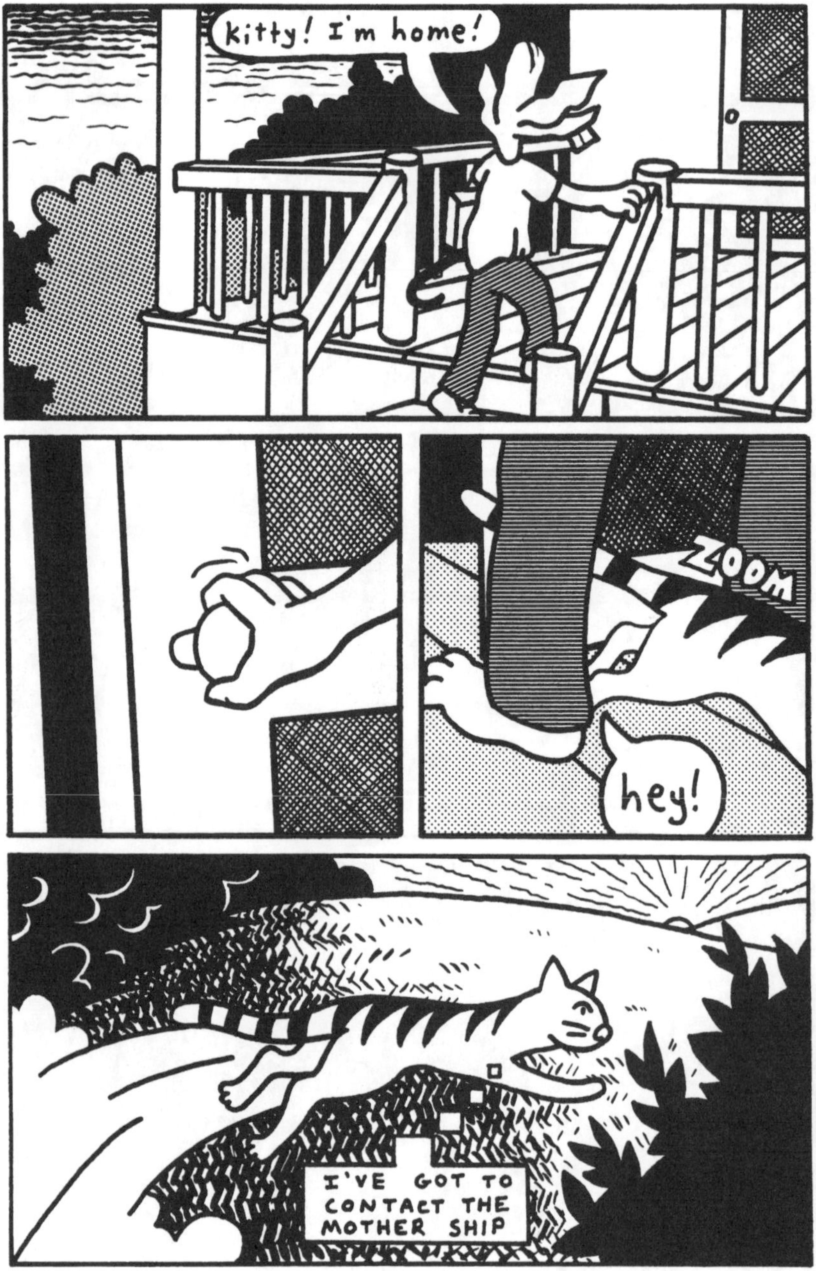
kitty! I'm home!
ZOOM
hey!
I'VE GOT TO CONTACT THE MOTHER SHIP

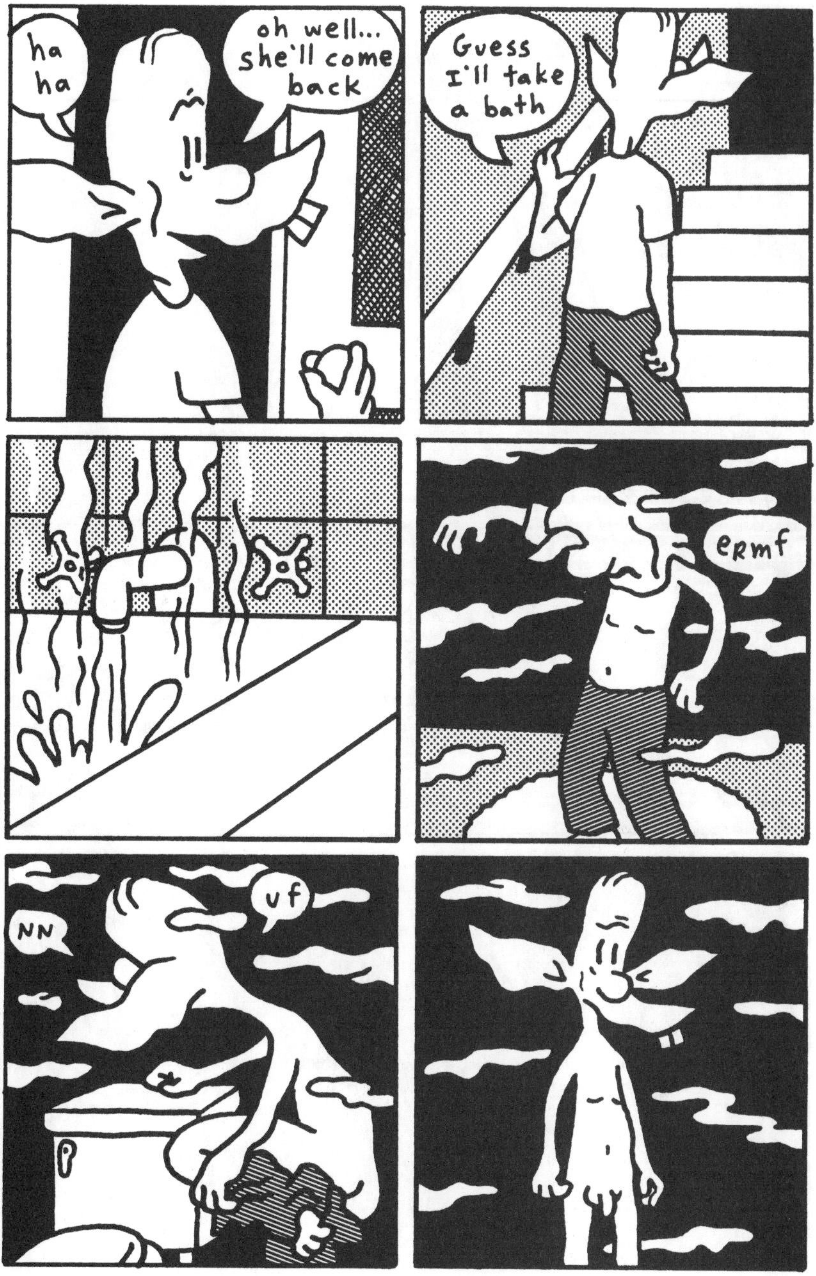
ha ha
oh well... she'll come back
Guess I'll take a bath
eRmf
NN
uf

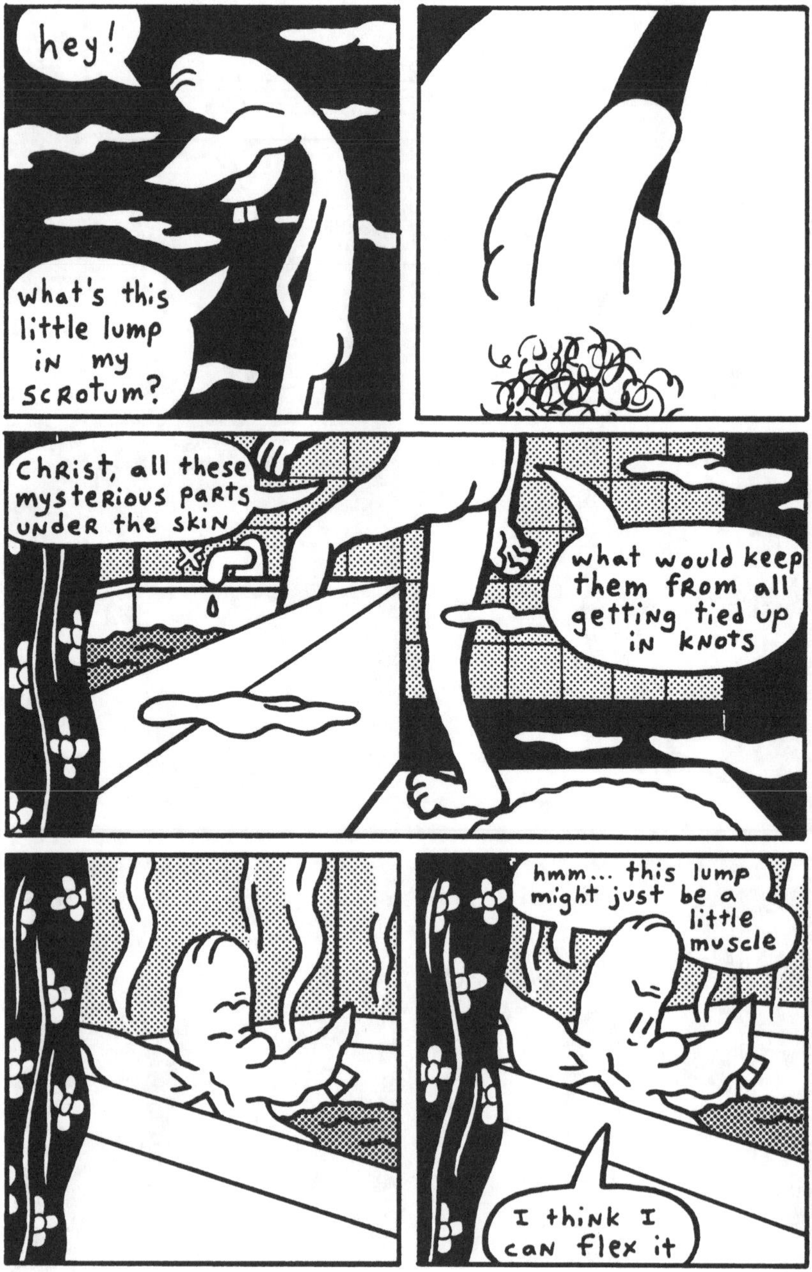
hey!
what's this little lump in my scrotum?
Christ, all these mysterious parts under the skin
what would keep them from all getting tied up in knots
hmm... this lump might just be a little muscle
I think I can flex it

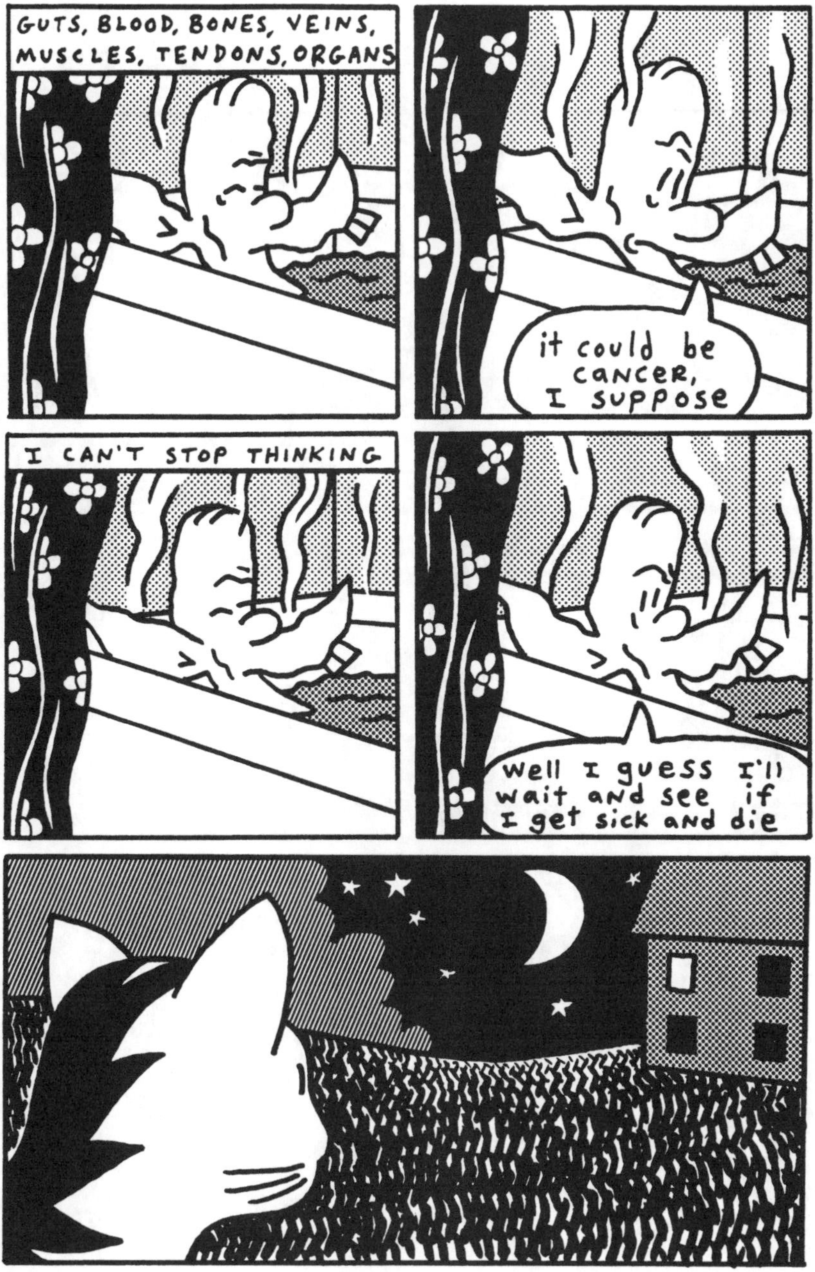
GUTS, BLOOD, BONES, VEINS, MUSCLES, TENDONS, ORGANS
it could be cancer, I suppose
I CAN'T STOP THINKING
well I guess I'll wait and see if I get sick and die

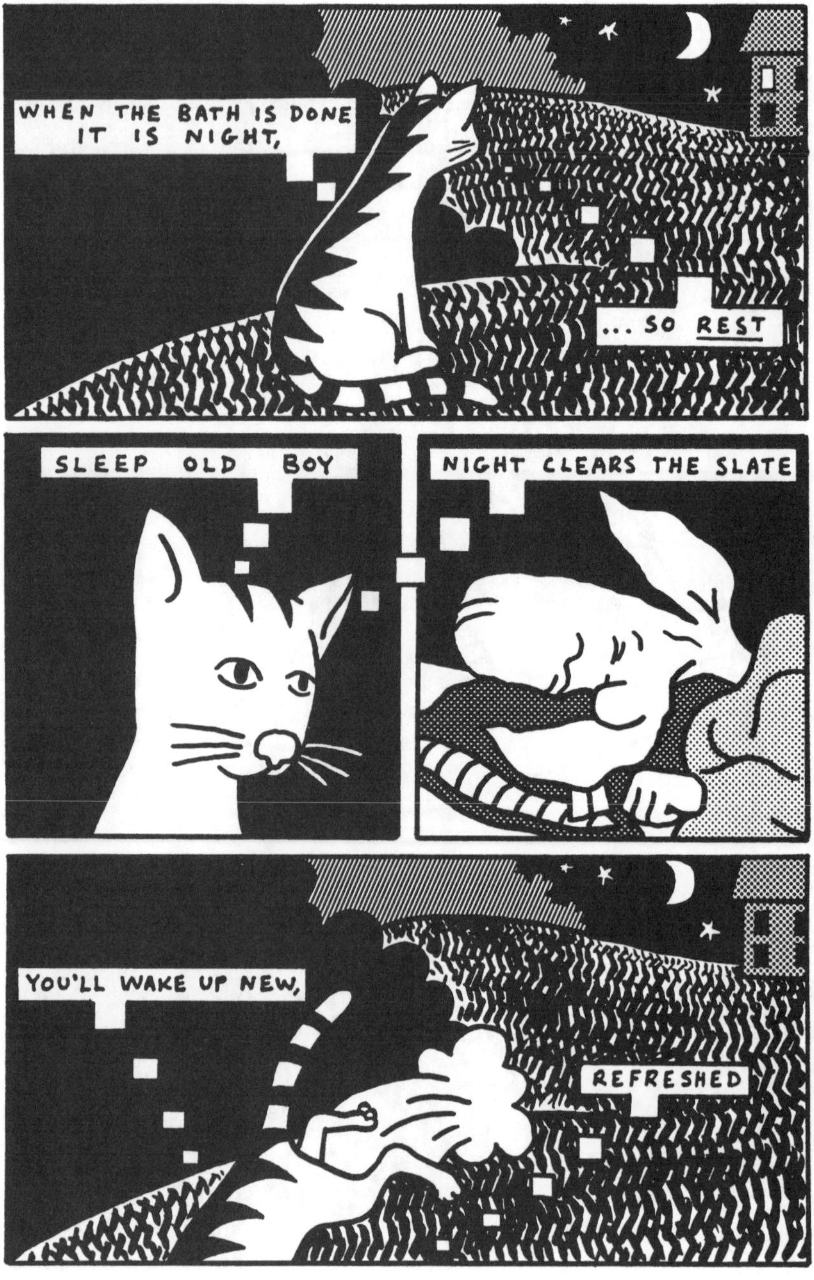
WHEN THE BATH IS DONE IT IS NIGHT,
... SO REST
SLEEP OLD BOY
NIGHT CLEARS THE SLATE
YOU'LL WAKE UP NEW,
REFRESHED

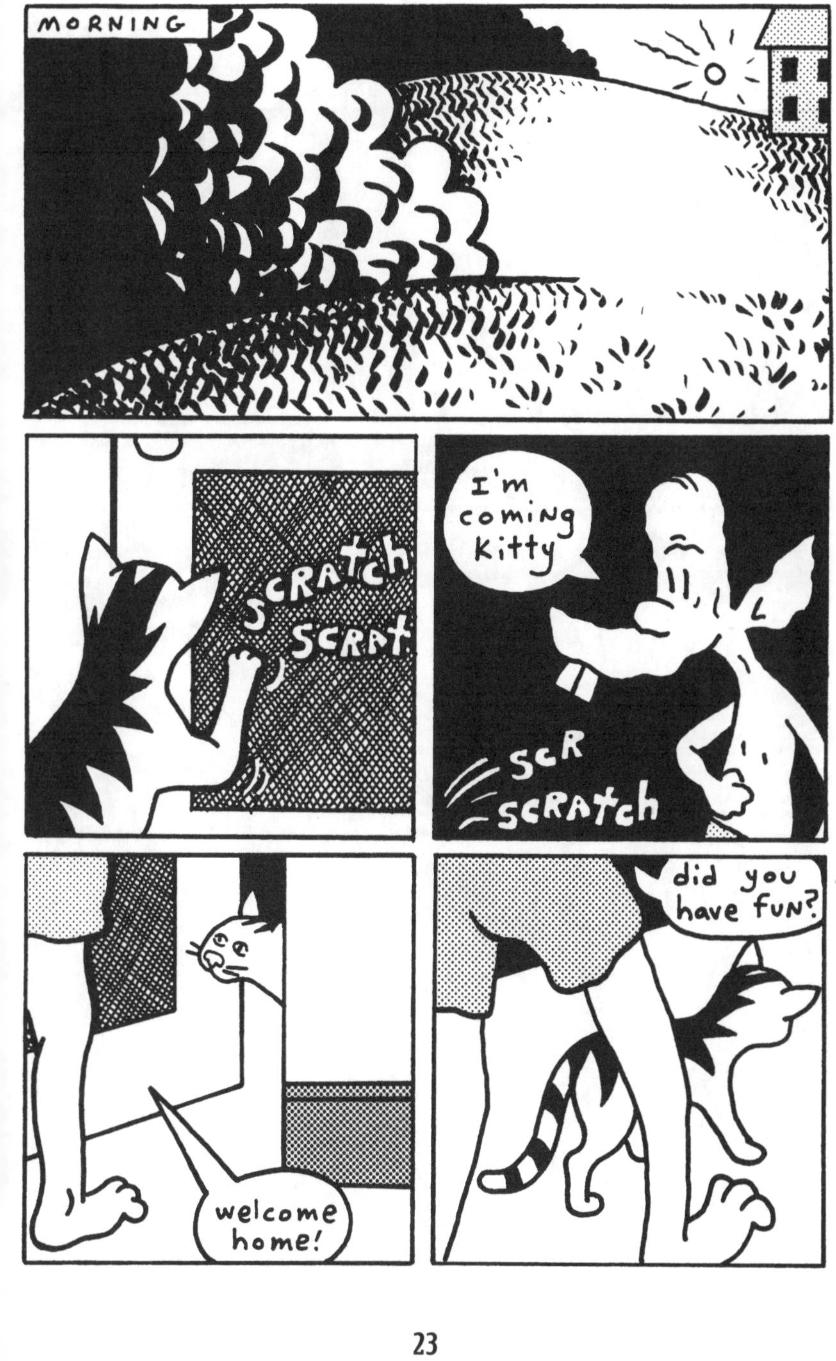
MORNING
SCRATCH
SCRAT
I'm coming kitty
SCR
SCRATCH
welcome home!
did you have fun?

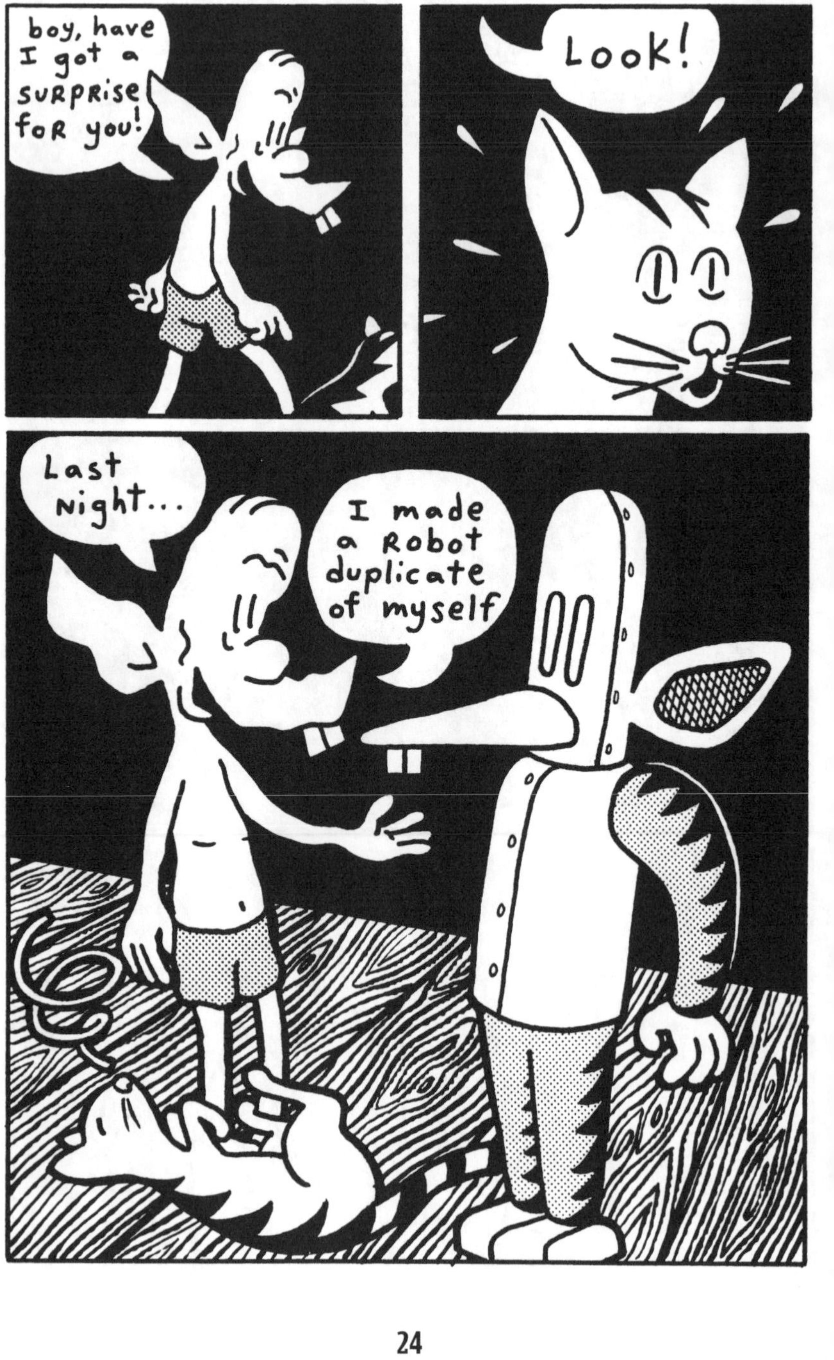
boy, have I got a SURPRISE FOR you!
LOOK!
Last Night...
I made a Robot duplicate of myself

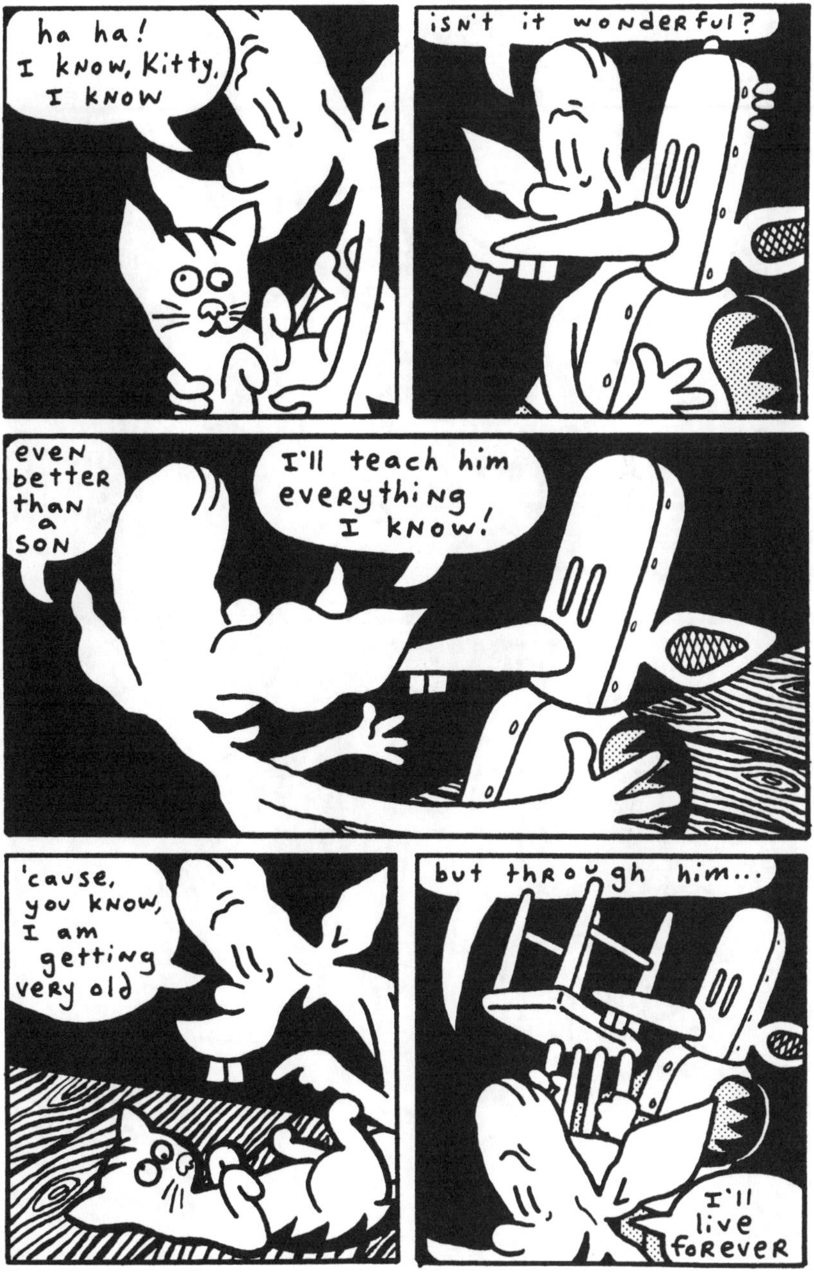
ha ha! I know, Kitty, I know
isn't it wonderful?
even better than a son
I'll teach him everything I know!
'cause, you know, I am getting very old
but through him...
I'll live forever

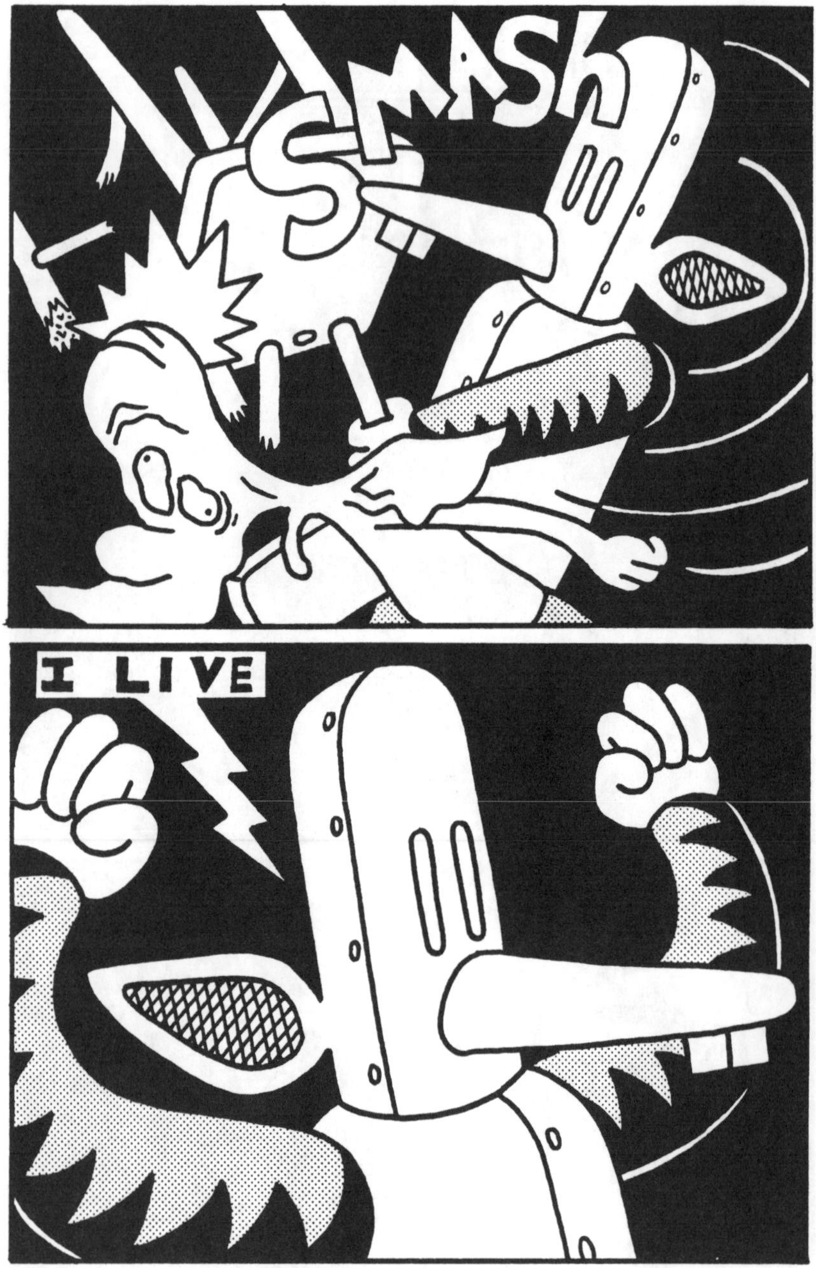
SMASH
I LIVE

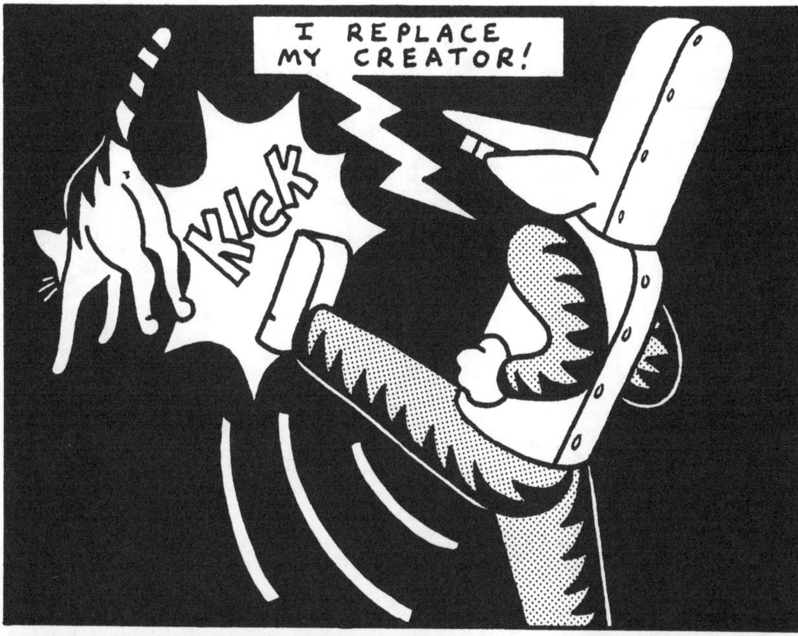
I REPLACE MY CREATOR!
KICK
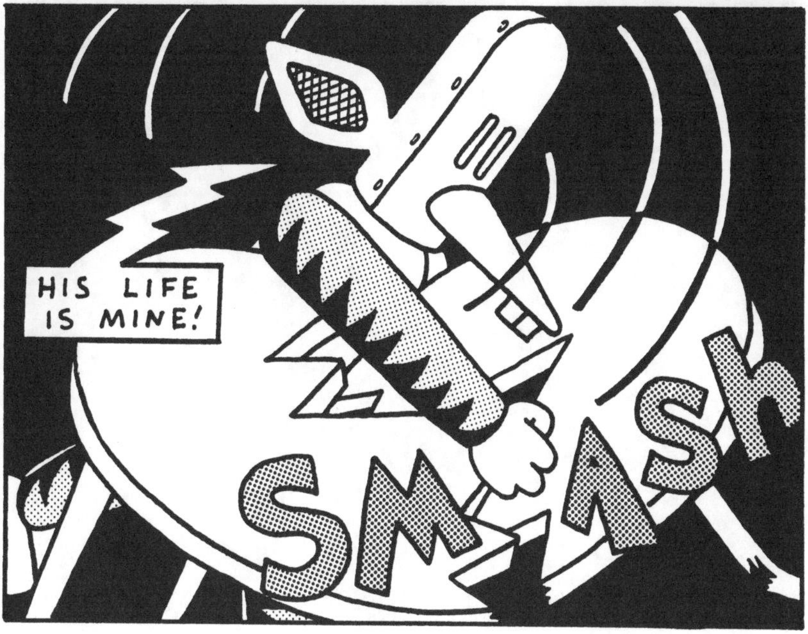
HIS LIFE IS MINE!
SMASH

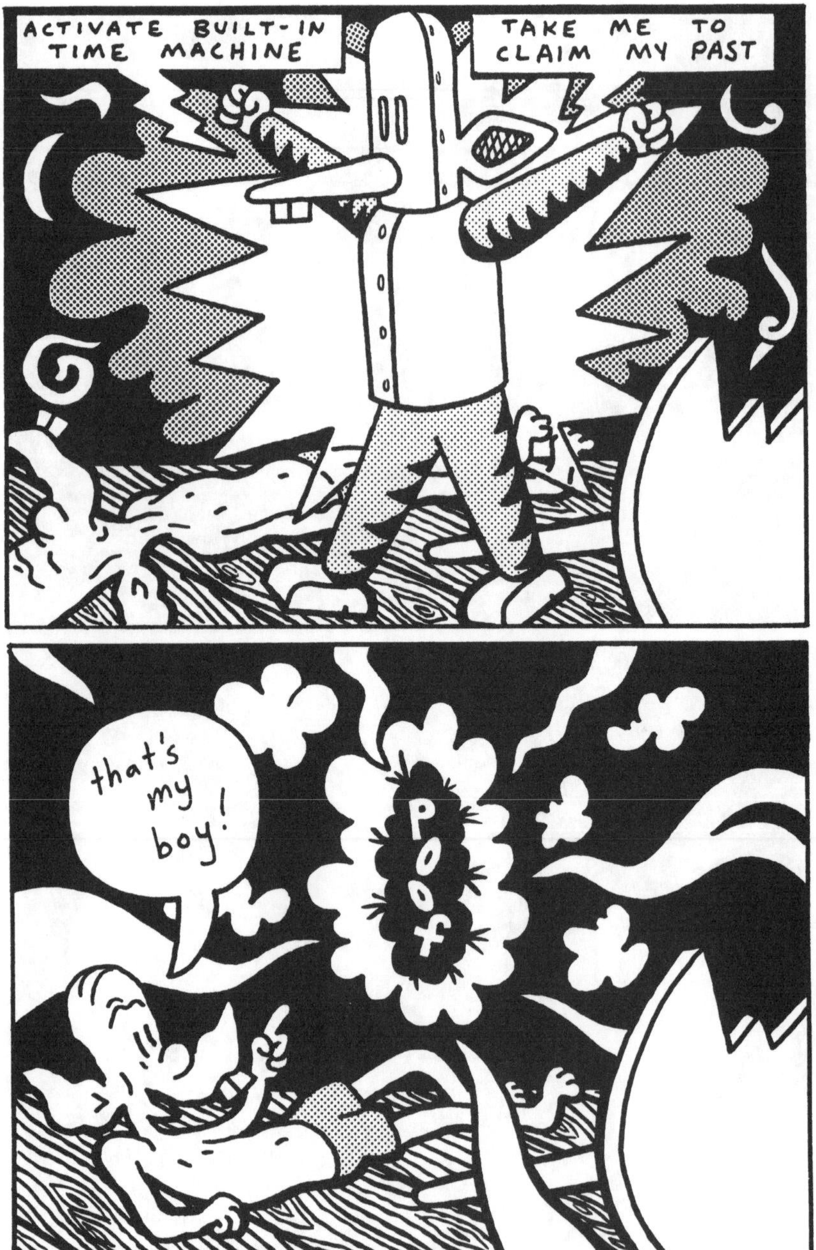
ACTIVATE BUILT-IN TIME MACHINE
TAKE ME TO CLAIM MY PAST
that's my boy!
POOF

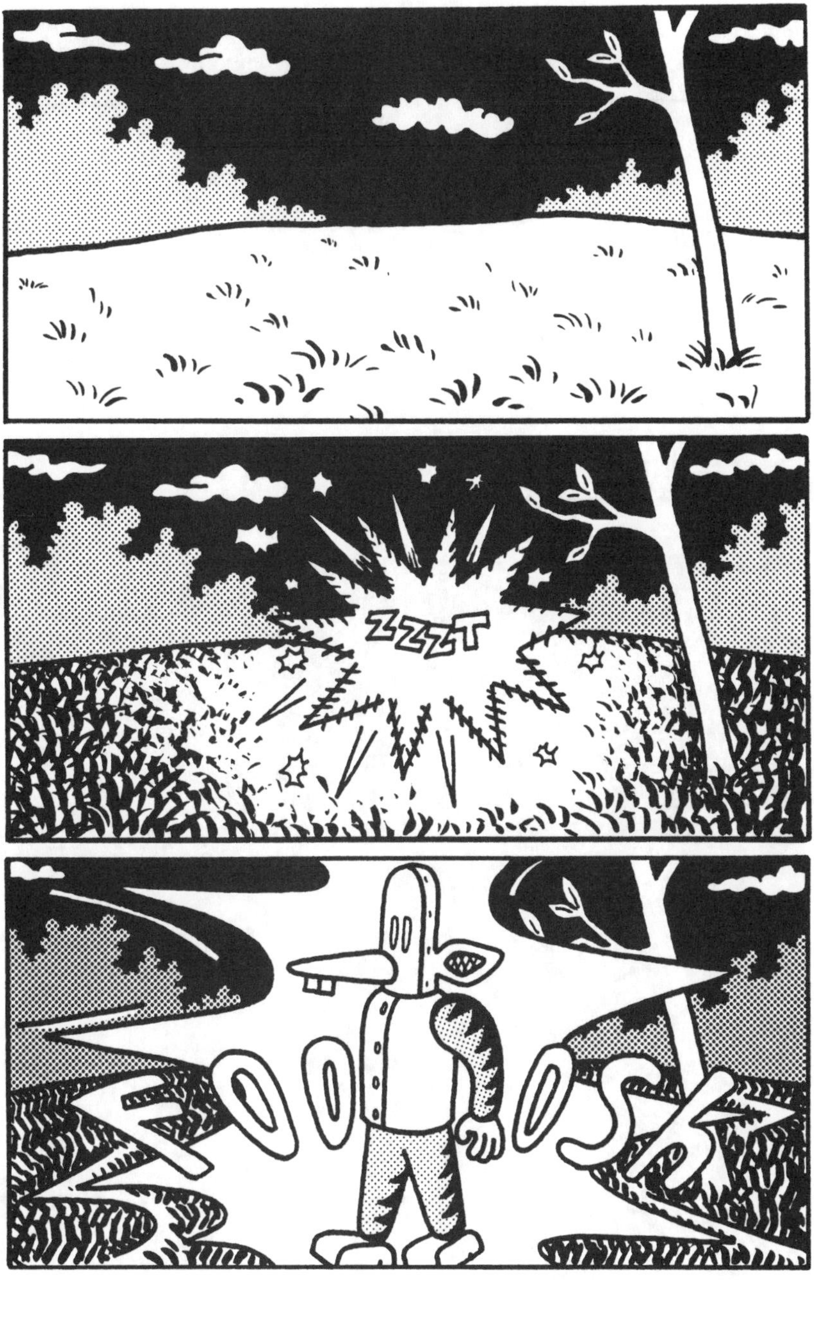
ZZZT
FOOOSH

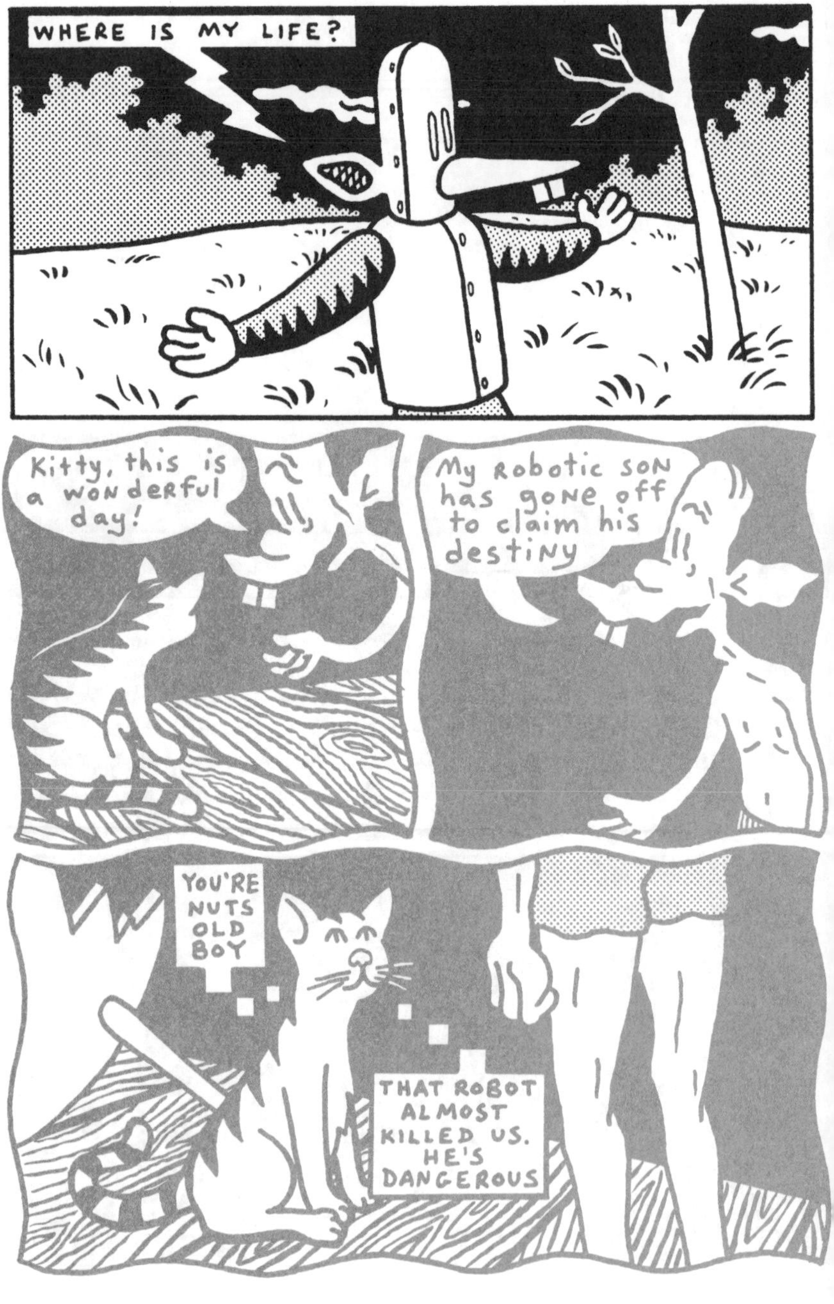

WHERE IS MY LIFE?
Kitty, this is a wonderful day!
My robotic son has gone off to claim his destiny
YOU'RE NUTS OLD BOY
THAT ROBOT ALMOST KILLED US. HE'S DANGEROUS

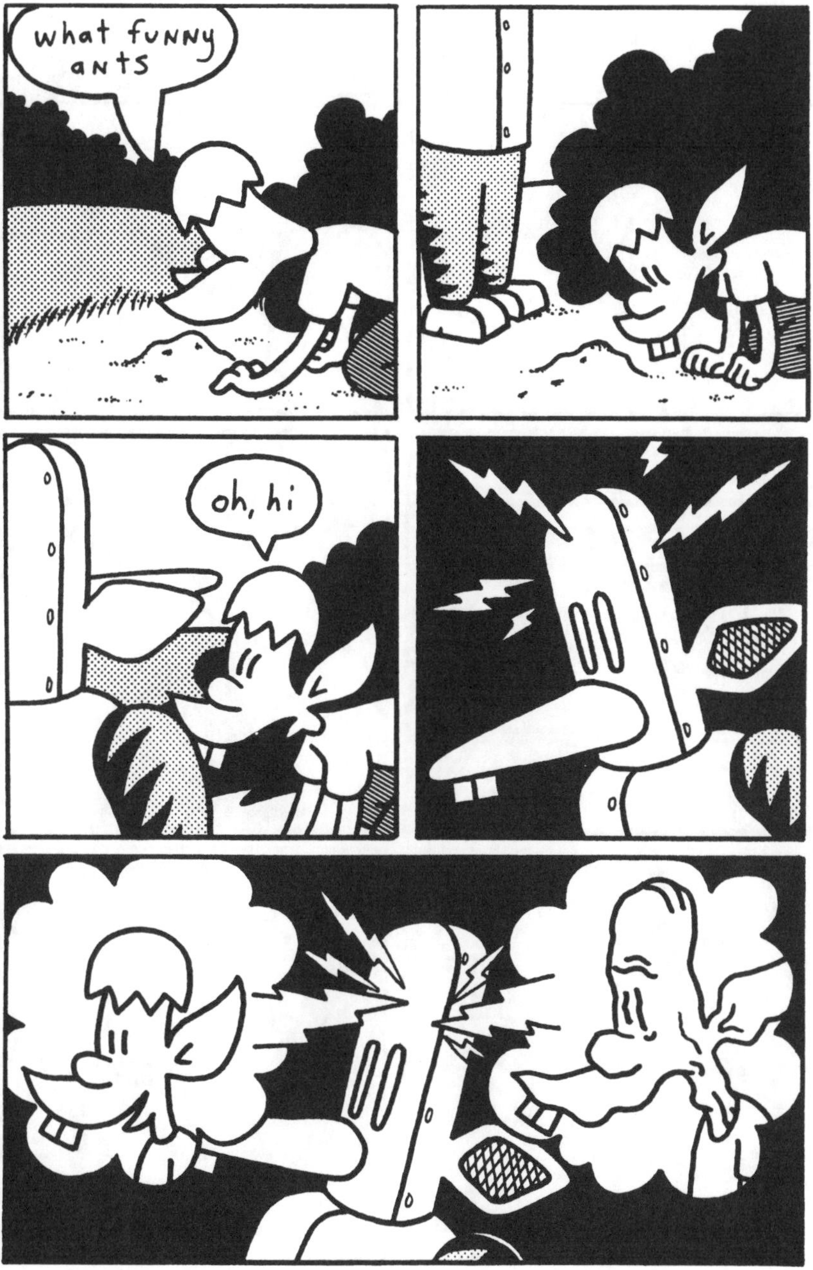
what funny ants
oh, hi

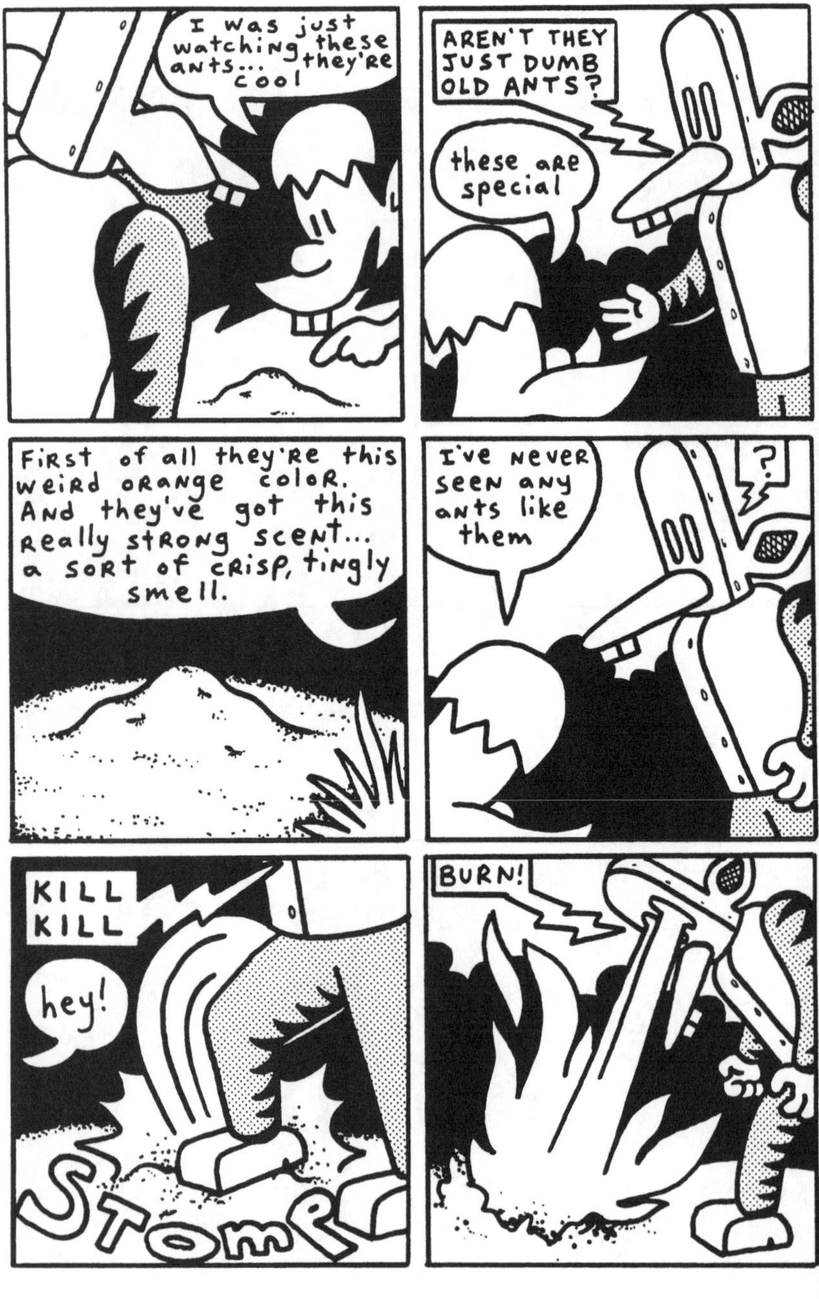
I was just watching these ants... they're cool
AREN'T THEY JUST DUMB OLD ANTS?
these are special
First of all they're this weird orange color. And they've got this really strong scent... a sort of crisp, tingly smell.
I've never seen any ants like them
?
KILL KILL
hey!
STOMP
BURN!

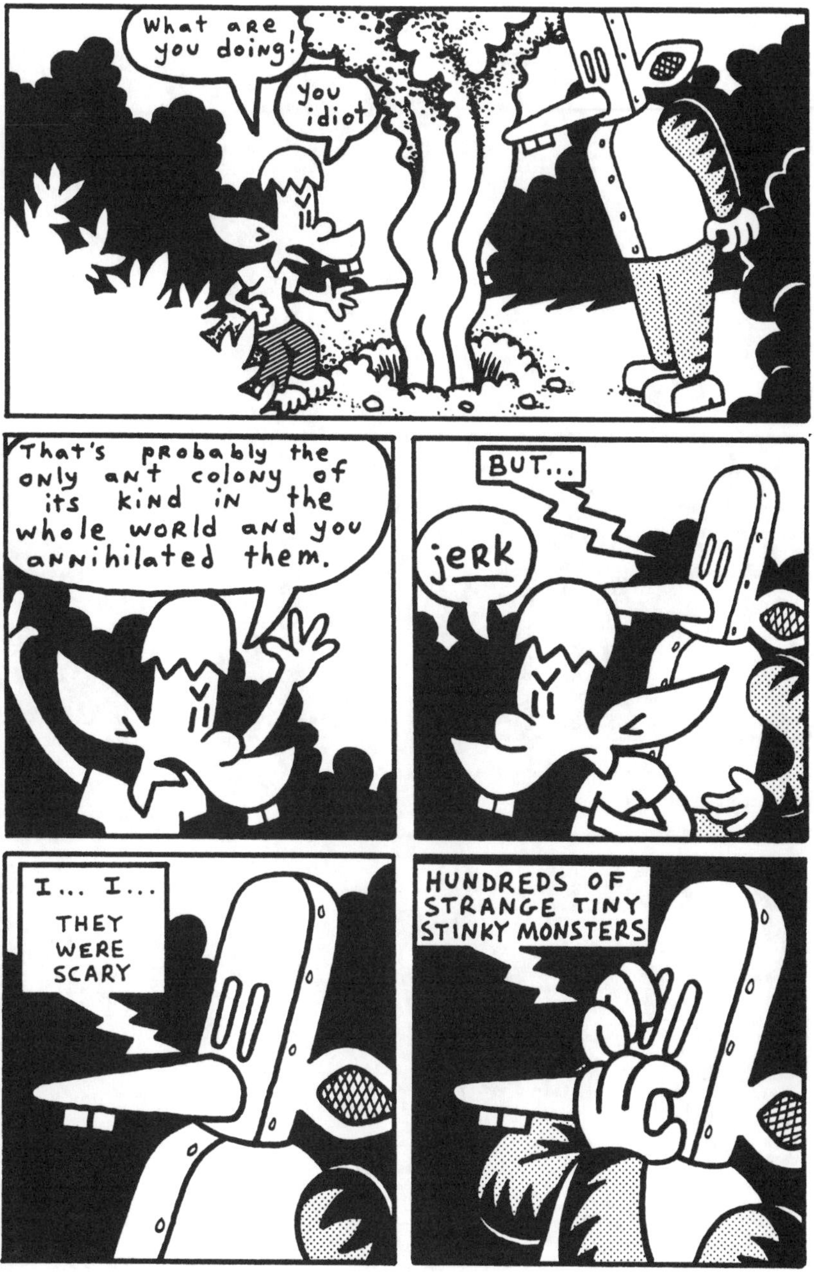
What are you doing!
you idiot
That's probably the only ant colony of its kind in the whole world and you annihilated them.
BUT...
jerk
I... I... THEY WERE SCARY
HUNDREDS OF STRANGE TINY STINKY MONSTERS

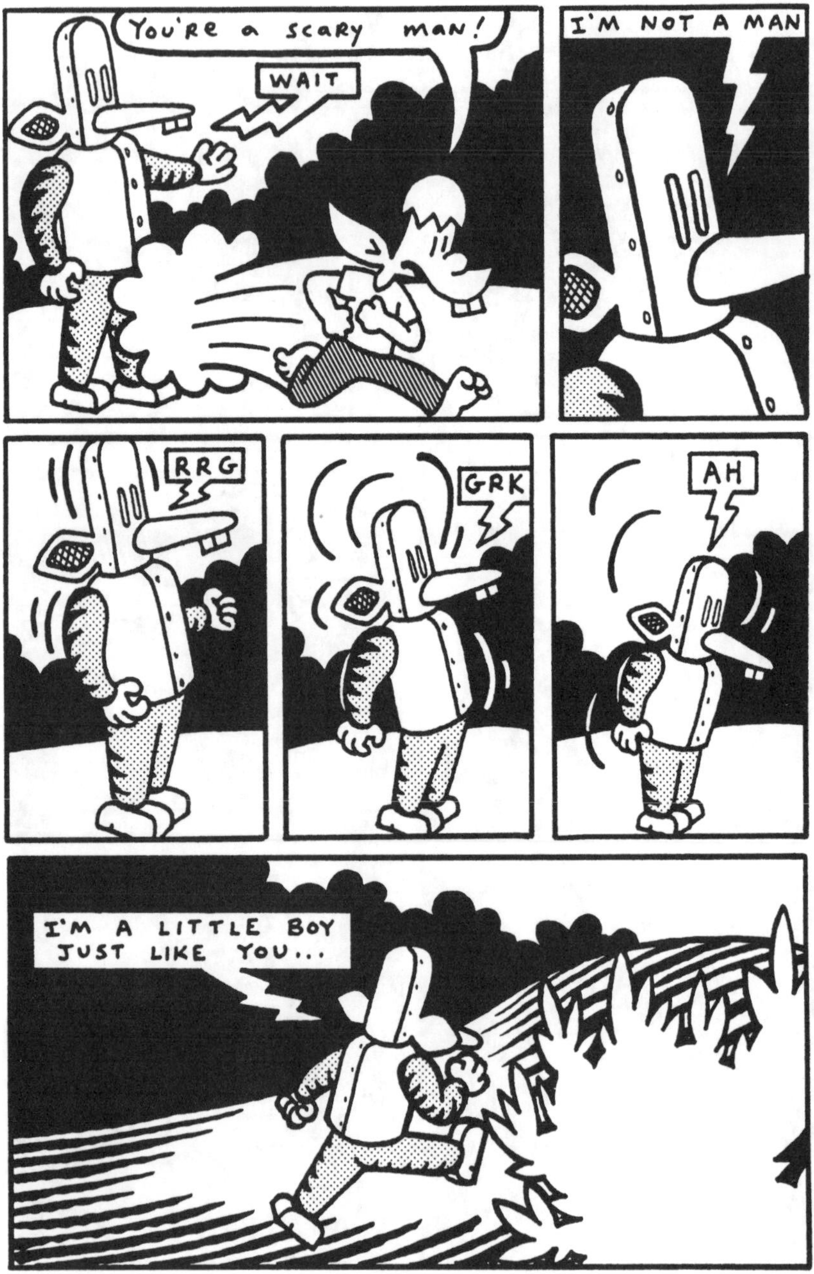
You're a scary man!
WAIT
I'M NOT A MAN
RRG
GRK
AH
I'M A LITTLE BOY
JUST LIKE YOU...

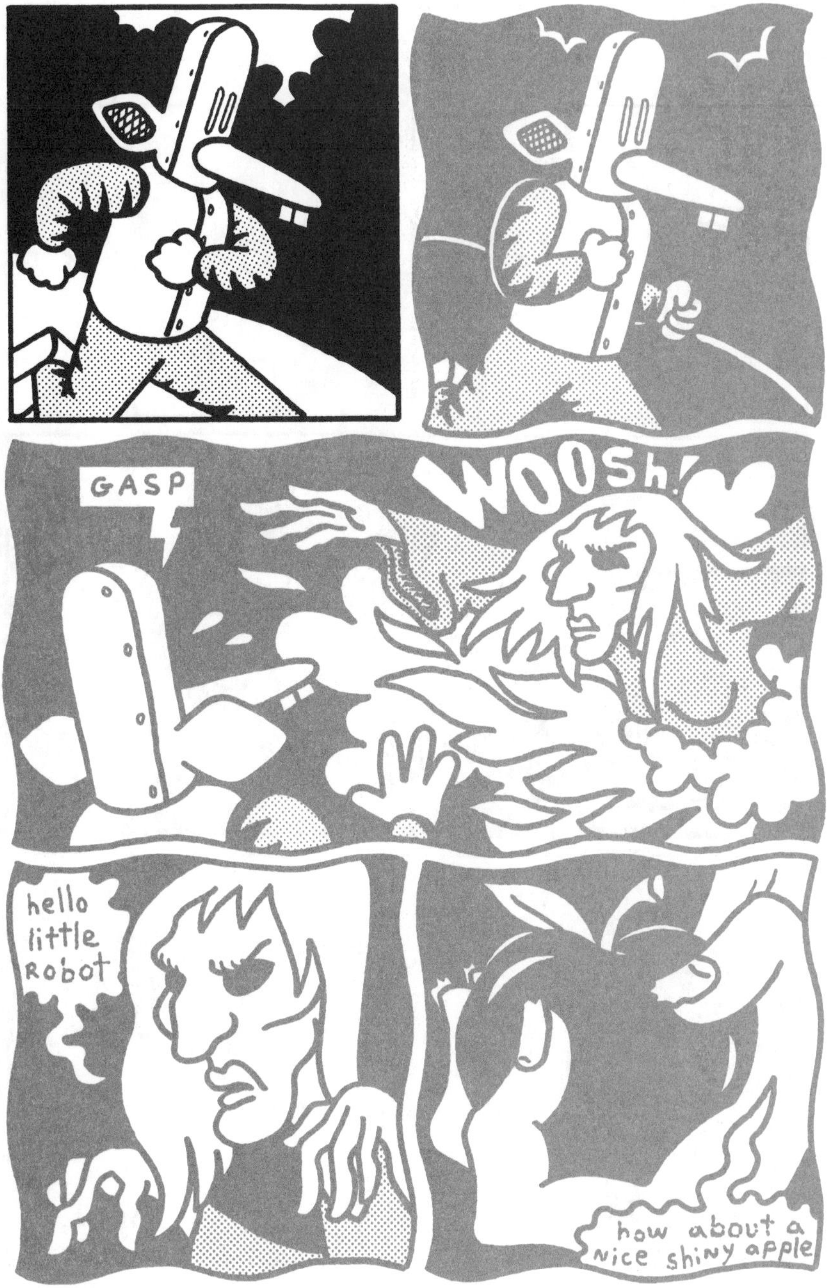
GASP
WOOSh!
hello little robot
how about a nice shiny apple

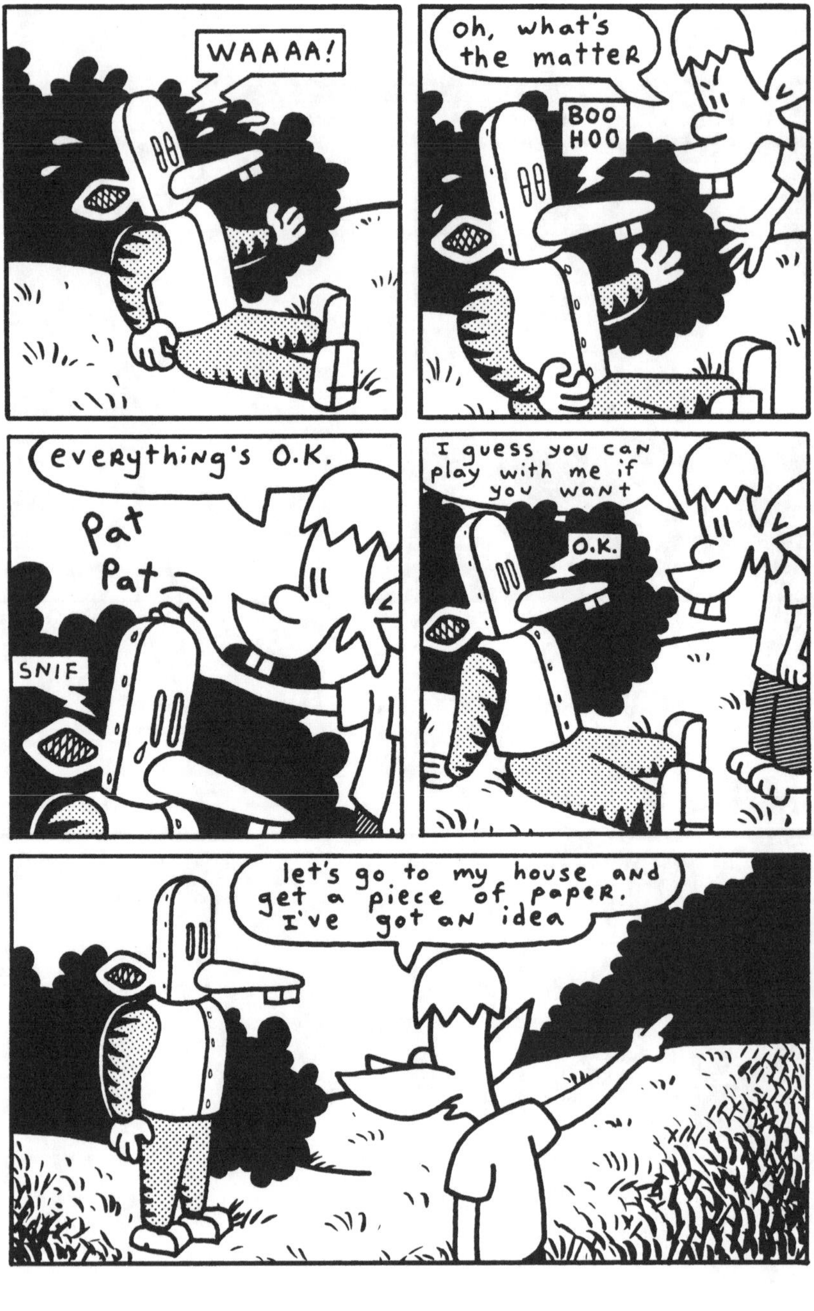
WAAAA!
Oh, what's the matter
BOO HOO
everything's O.K.
Pat Pat
SNIF
I guess you can play with me if you want
O.K.
let's go to my house and get a piece of paper. I've got an idea

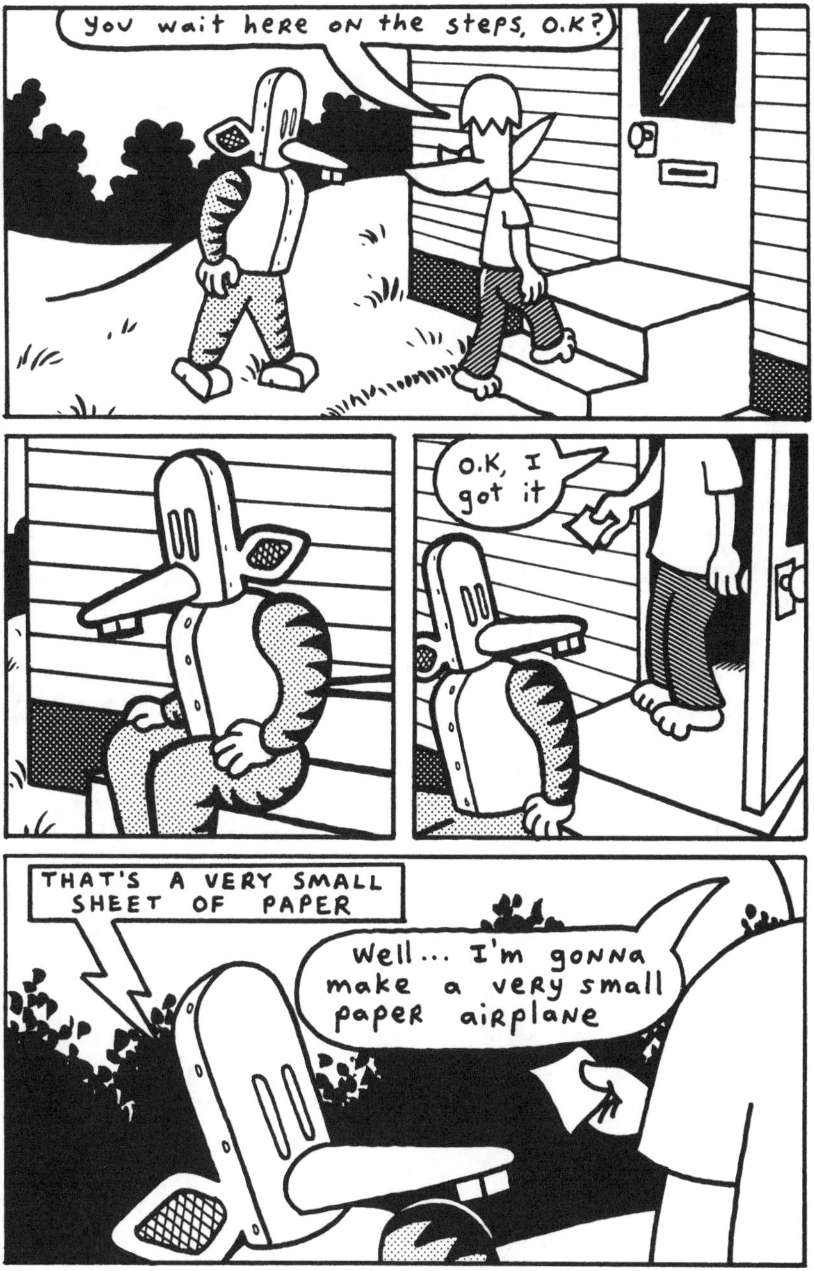
you wait here on the steps, O.K?
O.K, I got it
THAT'S A VERY SMALL SHEET OF PAPER
Well... I'm gonna make a very small paper airplane

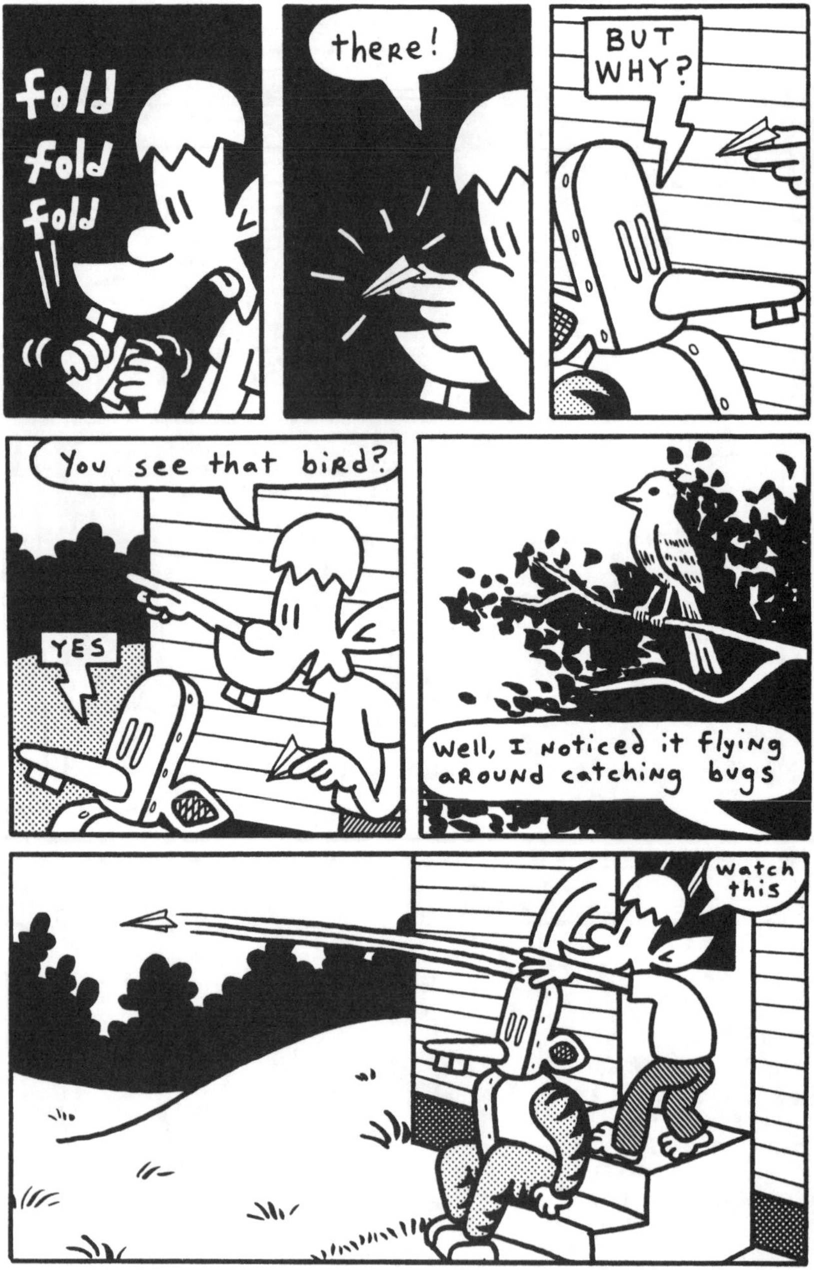
fold
fold
fold
there!
BUT WHY?
You see that bird?
YES
Well, I noticed it flying around catching bugs
watch this

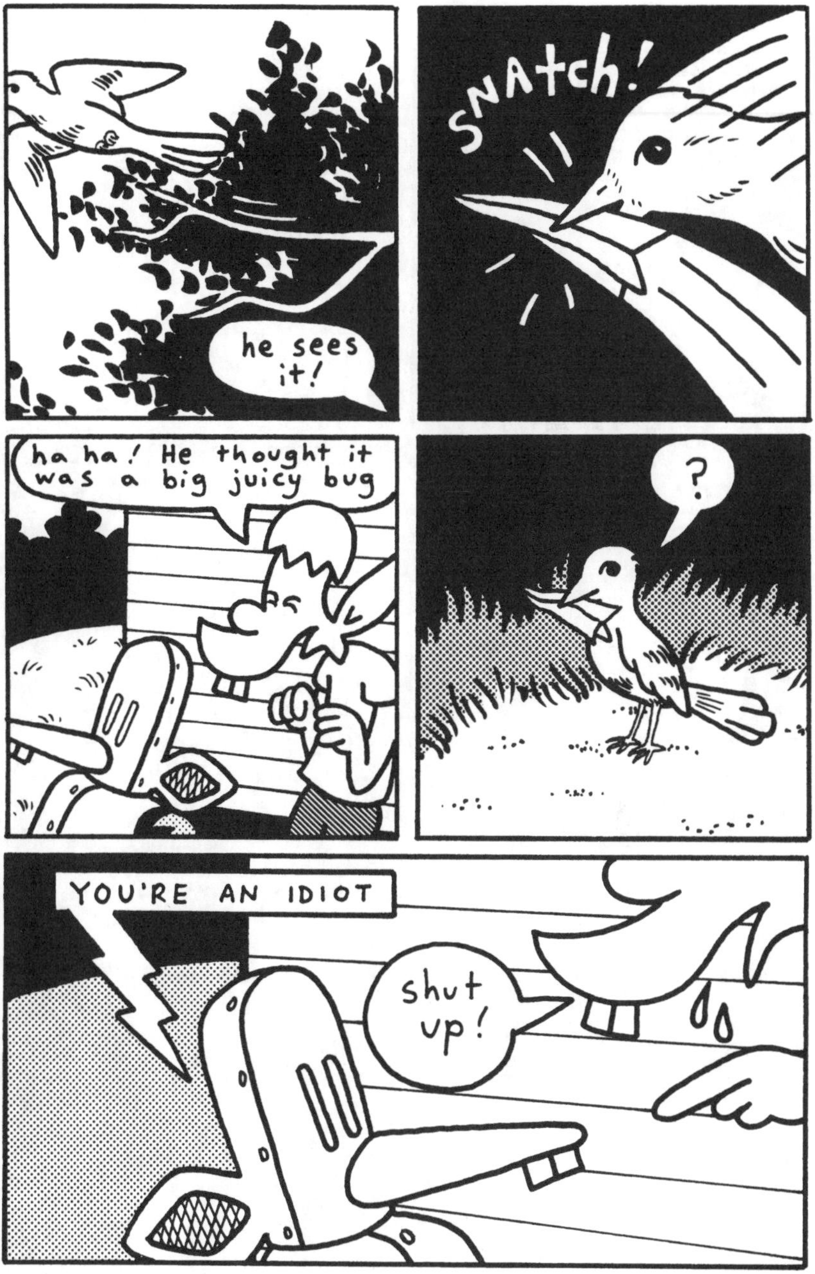
he sees it!
SNATCH!
ha ha! He thought it was a big juicy bug
?
YOU'RE AN IDIOT
shut up!

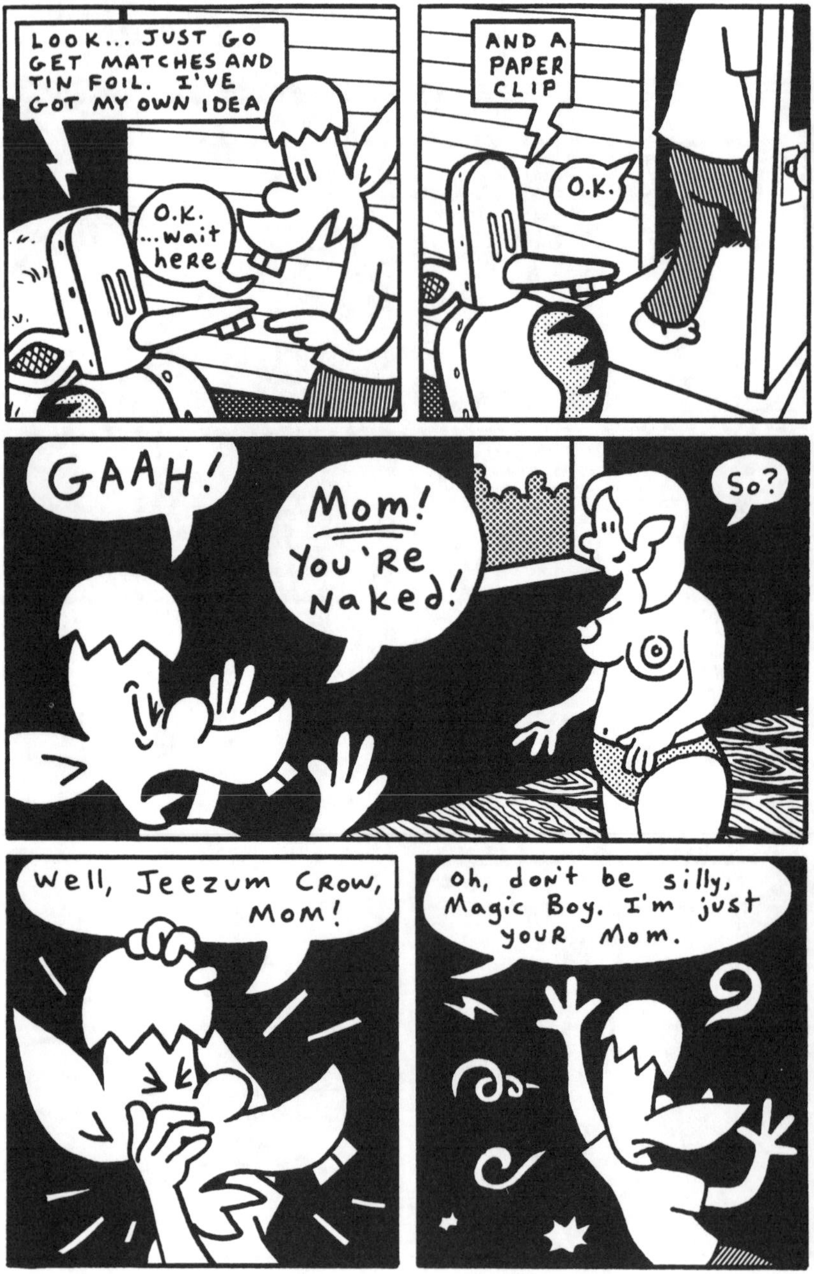
LOOK... JUST GO GET MATCHES AND TIN FOIL. I'VE GOT MY OWN IDEA
O.K. ...wait here
AND A PAPER CLIP
O.K.
GAAH!
Mom! You're naked!
So?
Well, Jeezum Crow, Mom!
Oh, don't be silly, Magic Boy. I'm just your Mom.

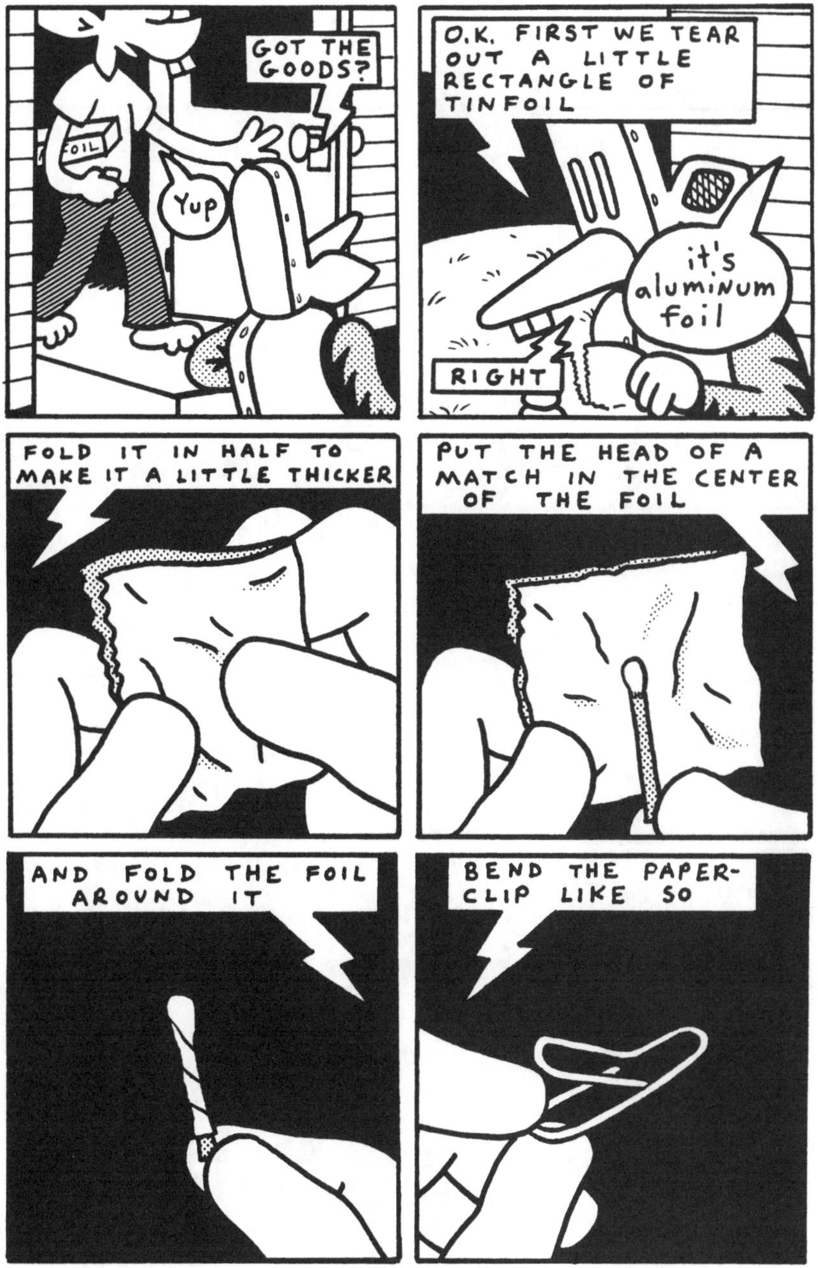
GOT THE GOODS?
YUP
FOIL
O.K. FIRST WE TEAR OUT A LITTLE RECTANGLE OF TINFOIL
it's aluminum foil
RIGHT
FOLD IT IN HALF TO MAKE IT A LITTLE THICKER
PUT THE HEAD OF A MATCH IN THE CENTER OF THE FOIL
AND FOLD THE FOIL AROUND IT
BEND THE PAPER-CLIP LIKE SO

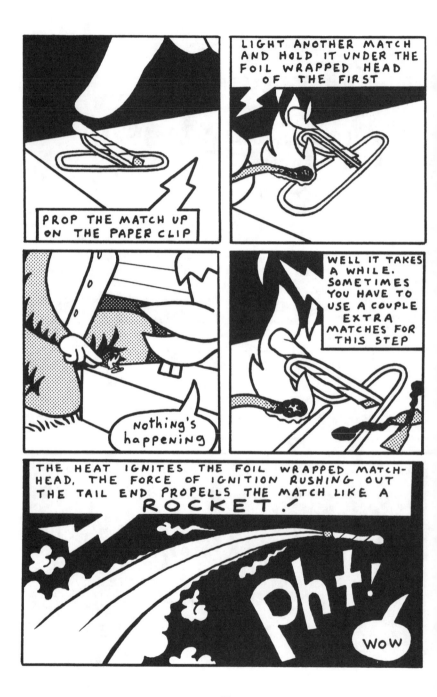

PROP THE MATCH UP ON THE PAPER CLIP

LIGHT ANOTHER MATCH AND HOLD IT UNDER THE FOIL WRAPPED HEAD OF THE FIRST

Nothing's happening

WELL IT TAKES A WHILE. SOMETIMES YOU HAVE TO USE A COUPLE EXTRA MATCHES FOR THIS STEP

THE HEAT IGNITES THE FOIL WRAPPED MATCH-HEAD, THE FORCE OF IGNITION RUSHING OUT THE TAIL END PROPELLS THE MATCH LIKE A ROCKET!

Pht!

WOW

42

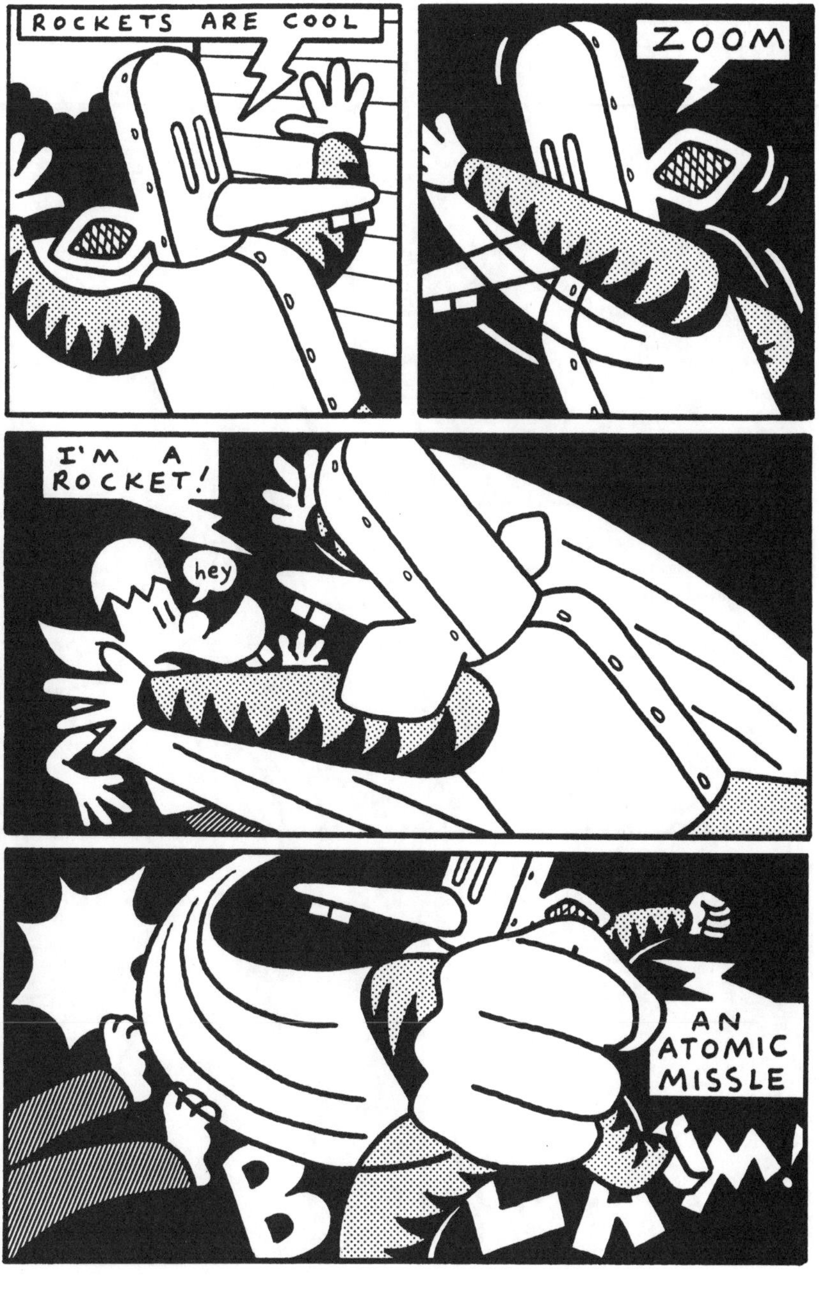
ROCKETS ARE COOL
ZOOM
I'M A ROCKET!
hey
AN ATOMIC MISSLE
BLAM!

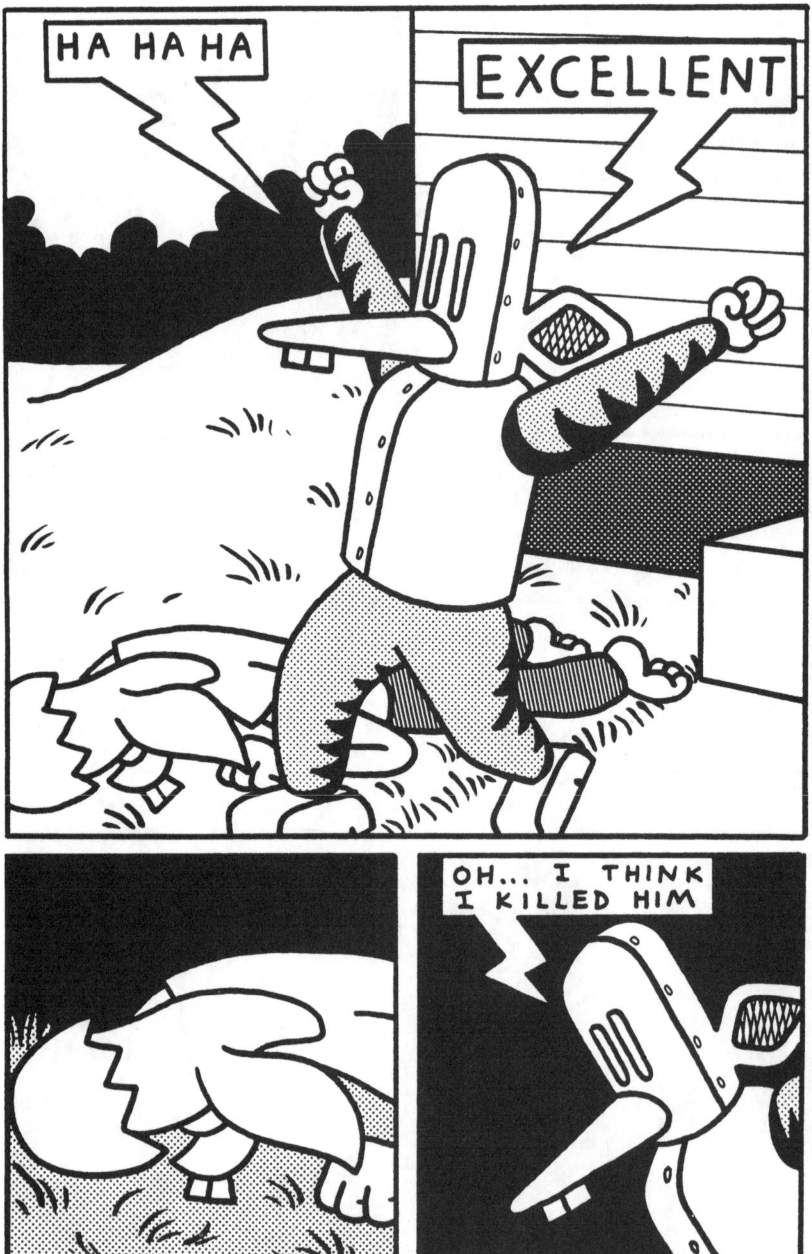
HA HA HA
EXCELLENT
OH... I THINK
I KILLED HIM

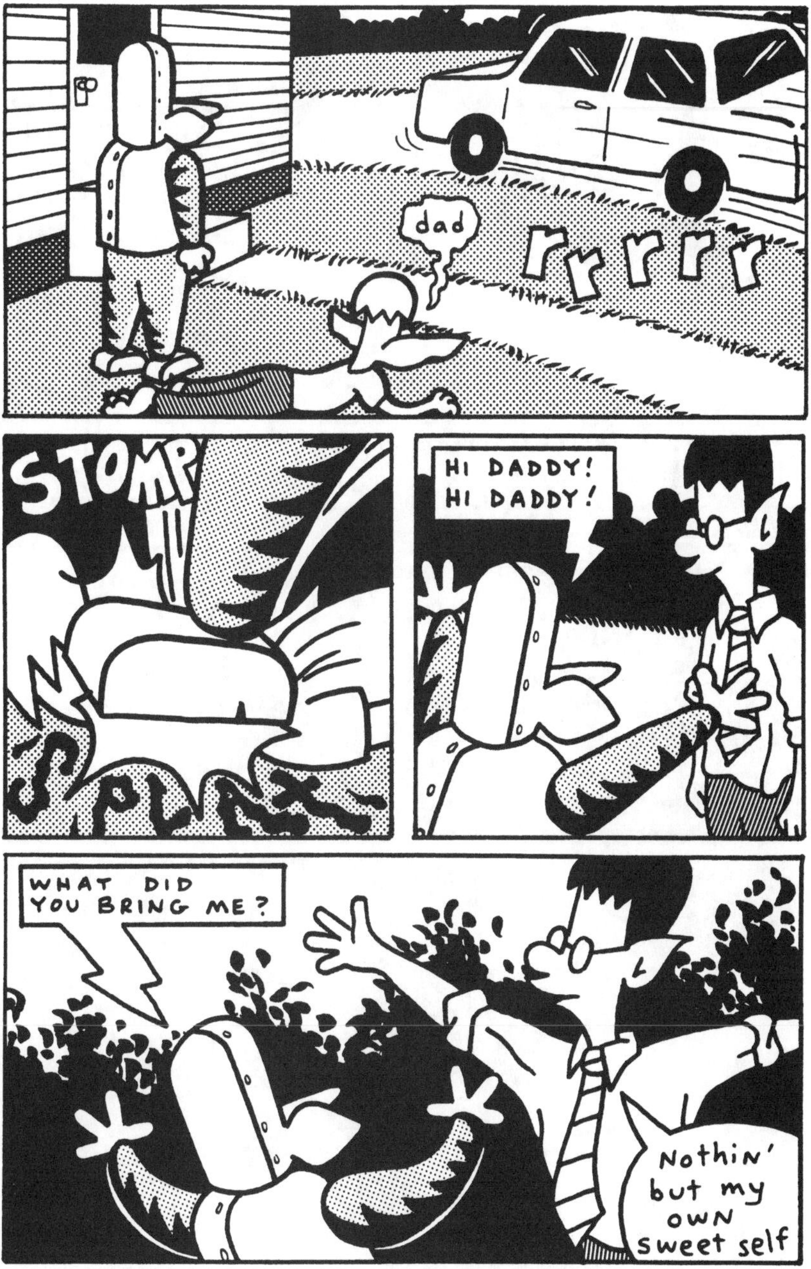
dad
rrrrr
STOMP
SPLAT
HI DADDY! HI DADDY!
WHAT DID YOU BRING ME?
Nothin' but my OWN sweet self

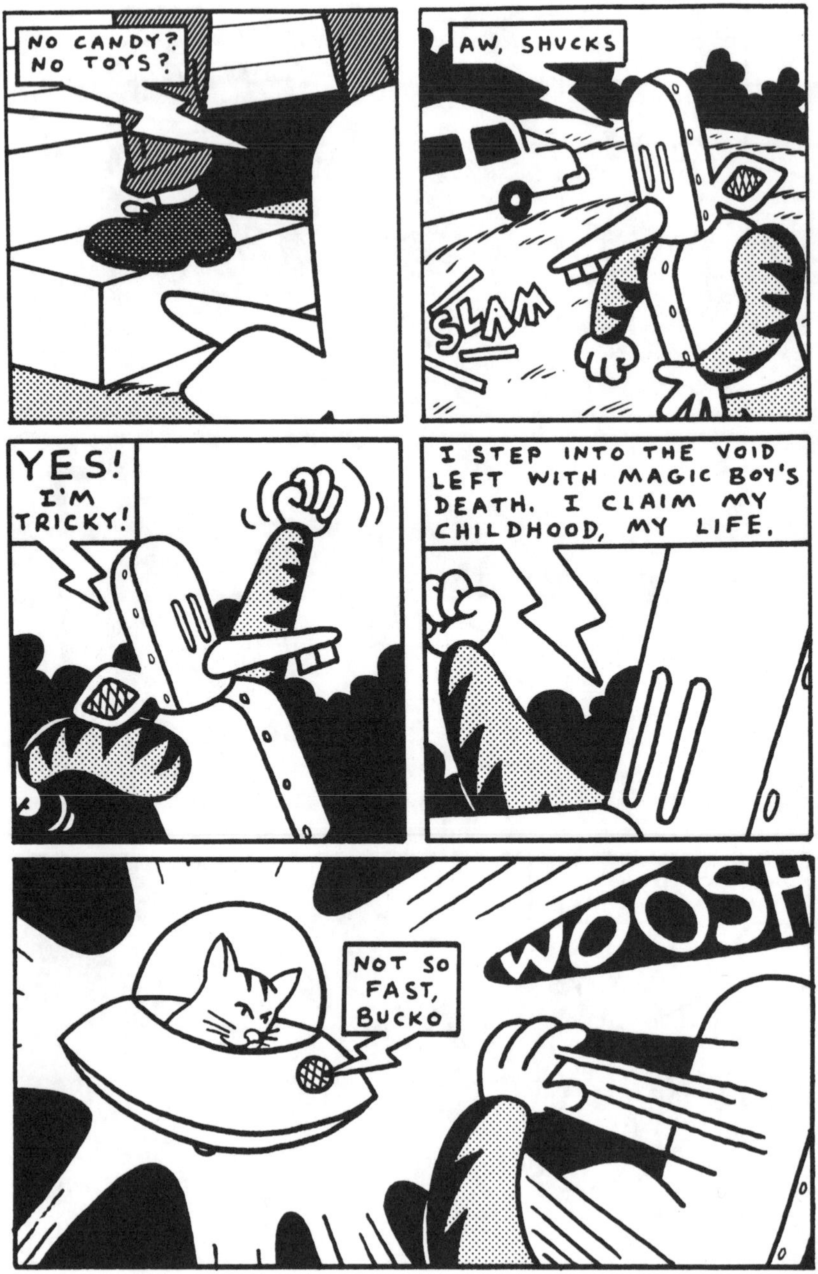
NO CANDY? NO TOYS?
AW, SHUCKS
SLAM
YES! I'M TRICKY!
I STEP INTO THE VOID LEFT WITH MAGIC BOY'S DEATH. I CLAIM MY CHILDHOOD, MY LIFE.
NOT SO FAST, BUCKO
WOOSH

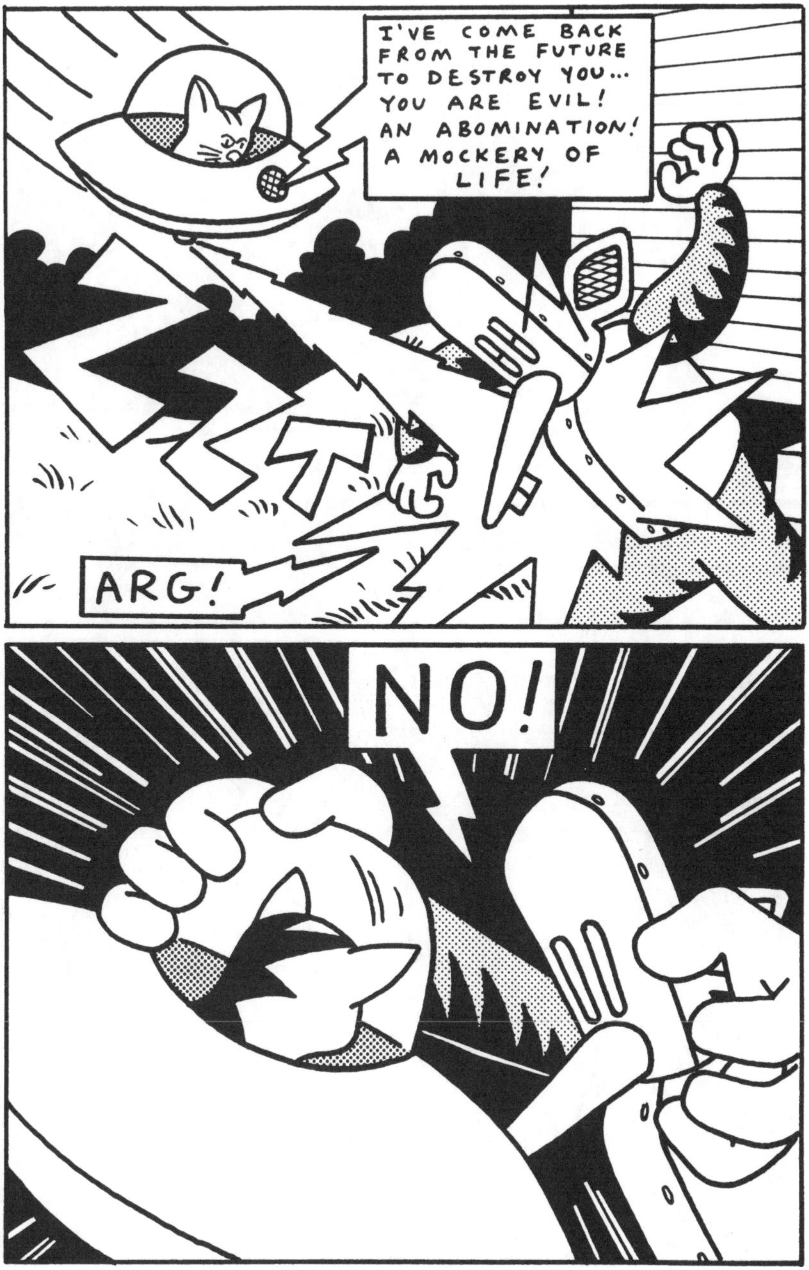
I'VE COME BACK FROM THE FUTURE TO DESTROY YOU... YOU ARE EVIL! AN ABOMINATION! A MOCKERY OF LIFE!
ZZZT
ARG!
NO!

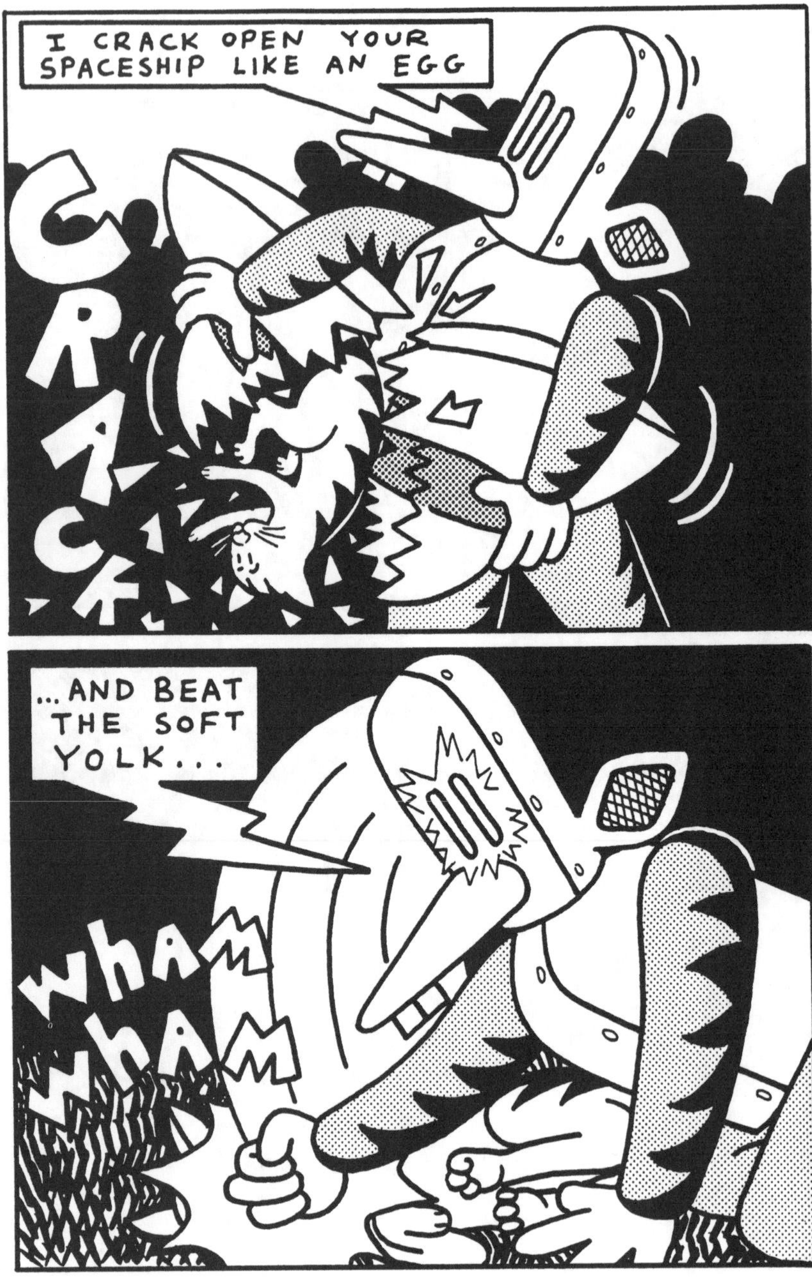
I CRACK OPEN YOUR SPACESHIP LIKE AN EGG
CRACK
...AND BEAT THE SOFT YOLK...
WHAM
WHAM

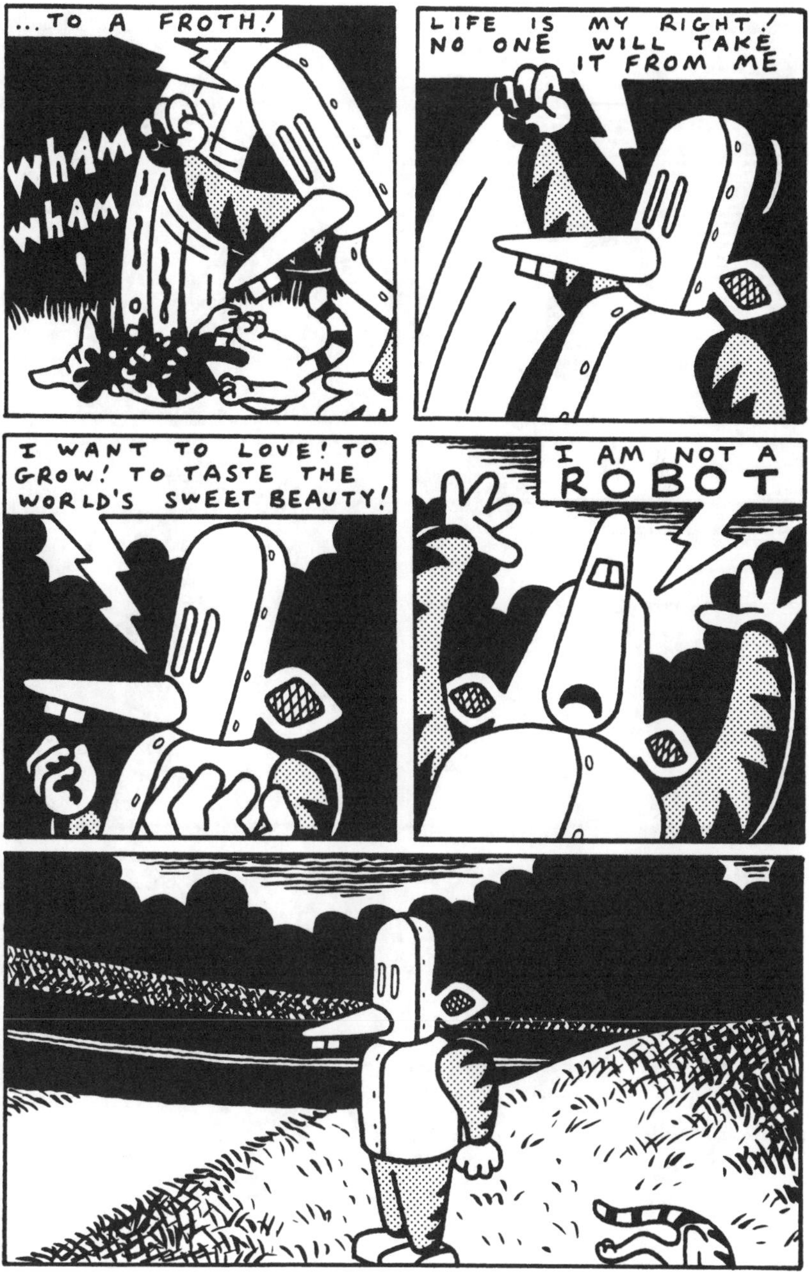
...TO A FROTH!
WHAM WHAM
LIFE IS MY RIGHT! NO ONE WILL TAKE IT FROM ME
I WANT TO LOVE! TO GROW! TO TASTE THE WORLD'S SWEET BEAUTY!
I AM NOT A ROBOT

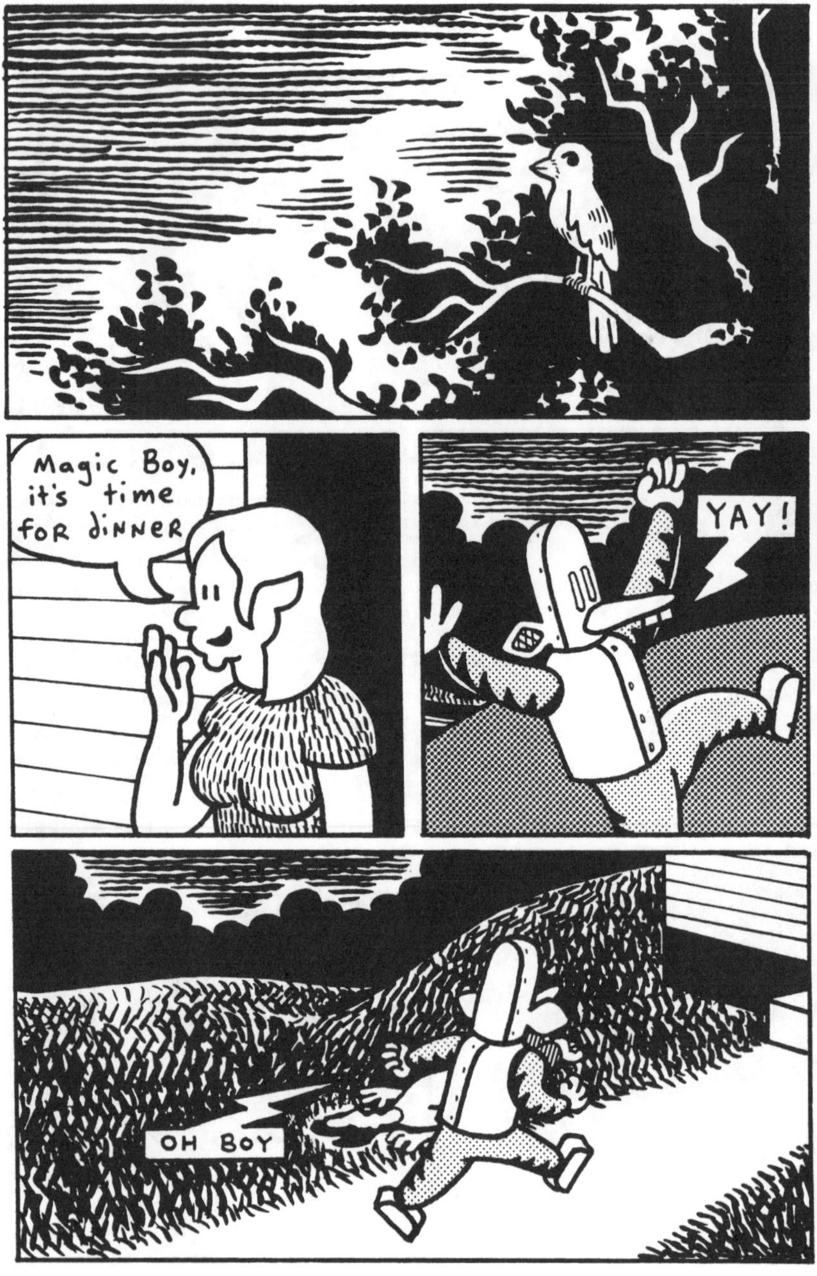
Magic Boy, it's time for dinner
YAY!
OH BOY

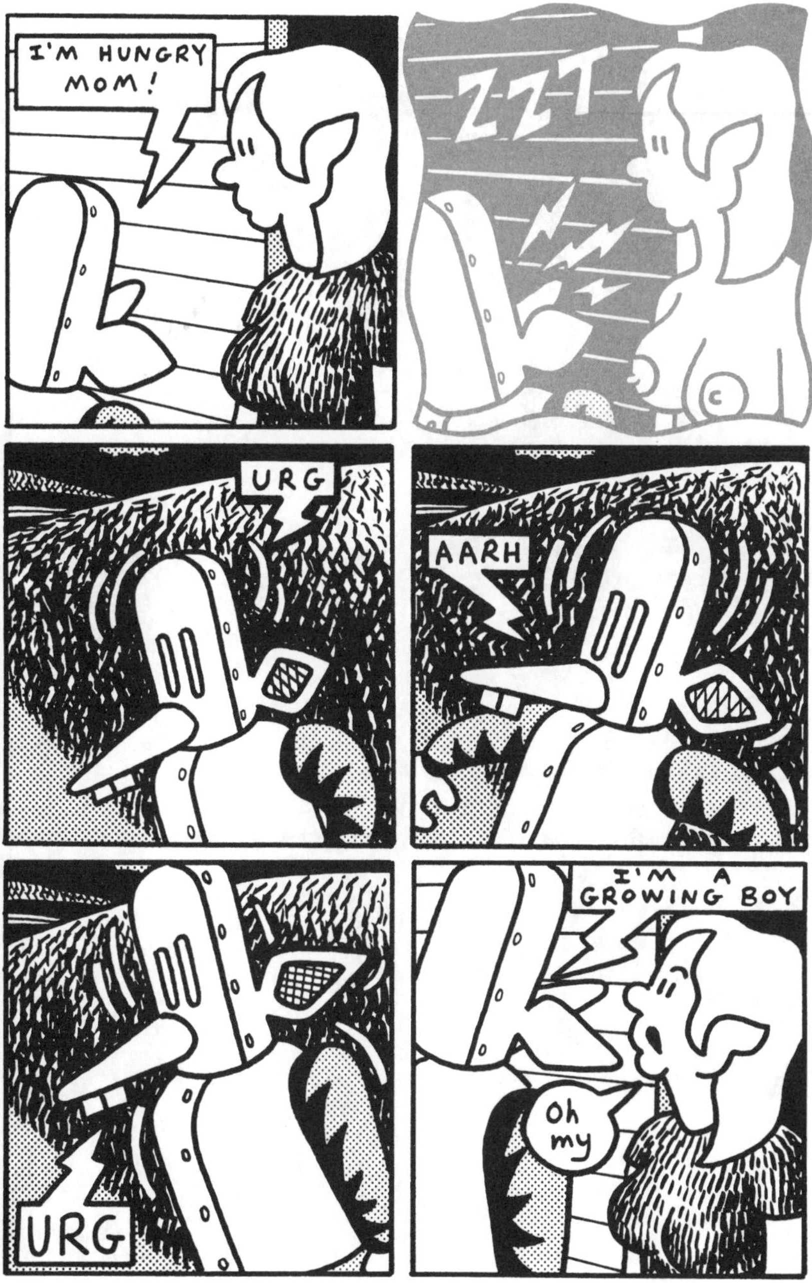
I'M HUNGRY MOM!
ZZT
URG
AARH
URG
I'M A GROWING BOY
Oh my

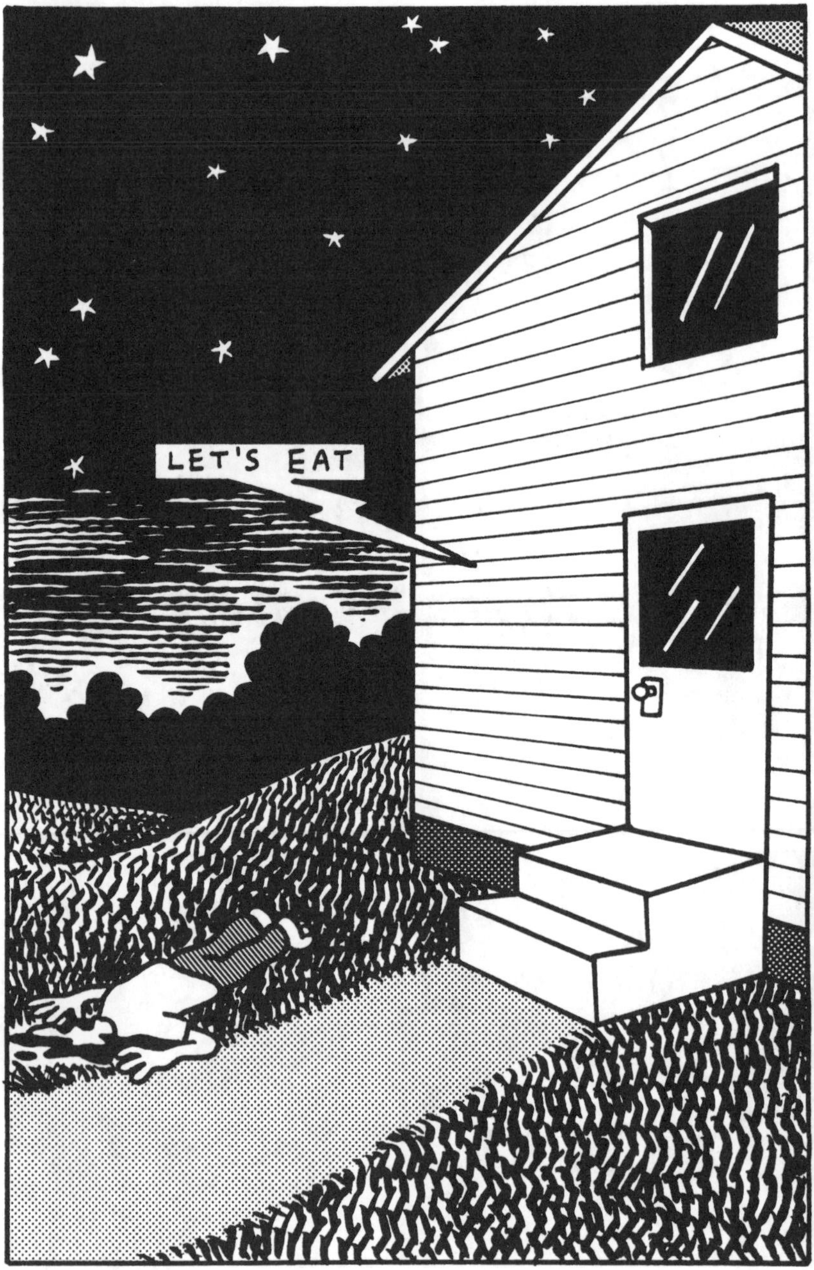
LET'S EAT

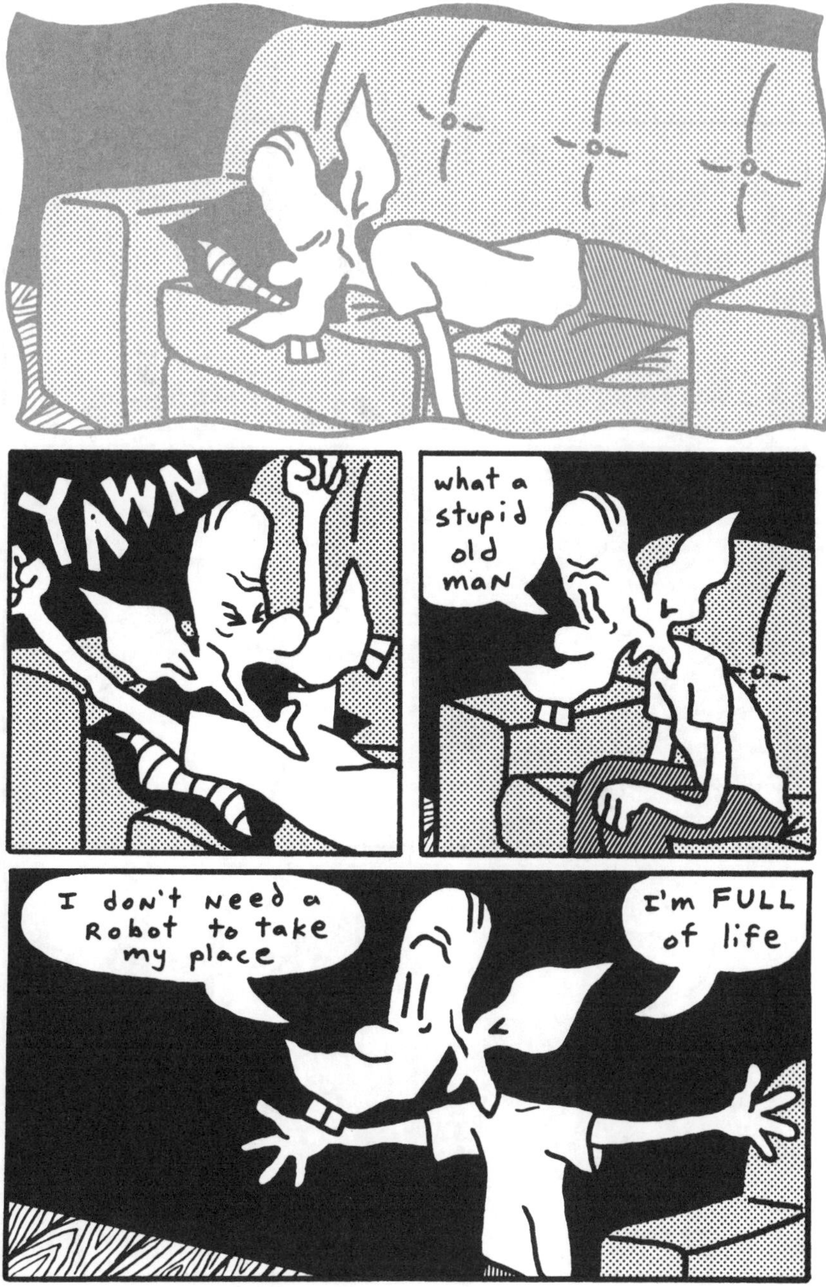
YAWN
what a stupid old man
I don't need a Robot to take my place
I'm FULL of life

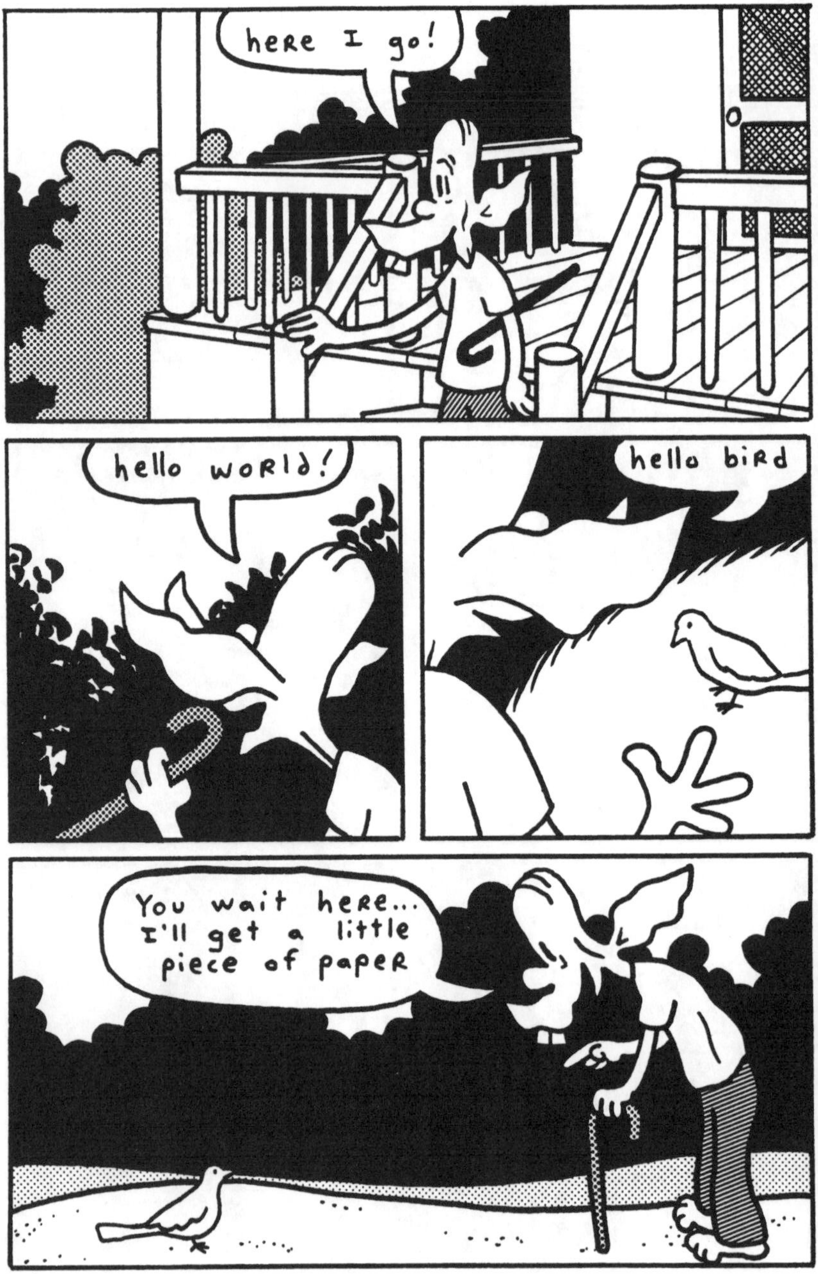
here I go!
hello world!
hello bird
You wait here...
I'll get a little
piece of paper

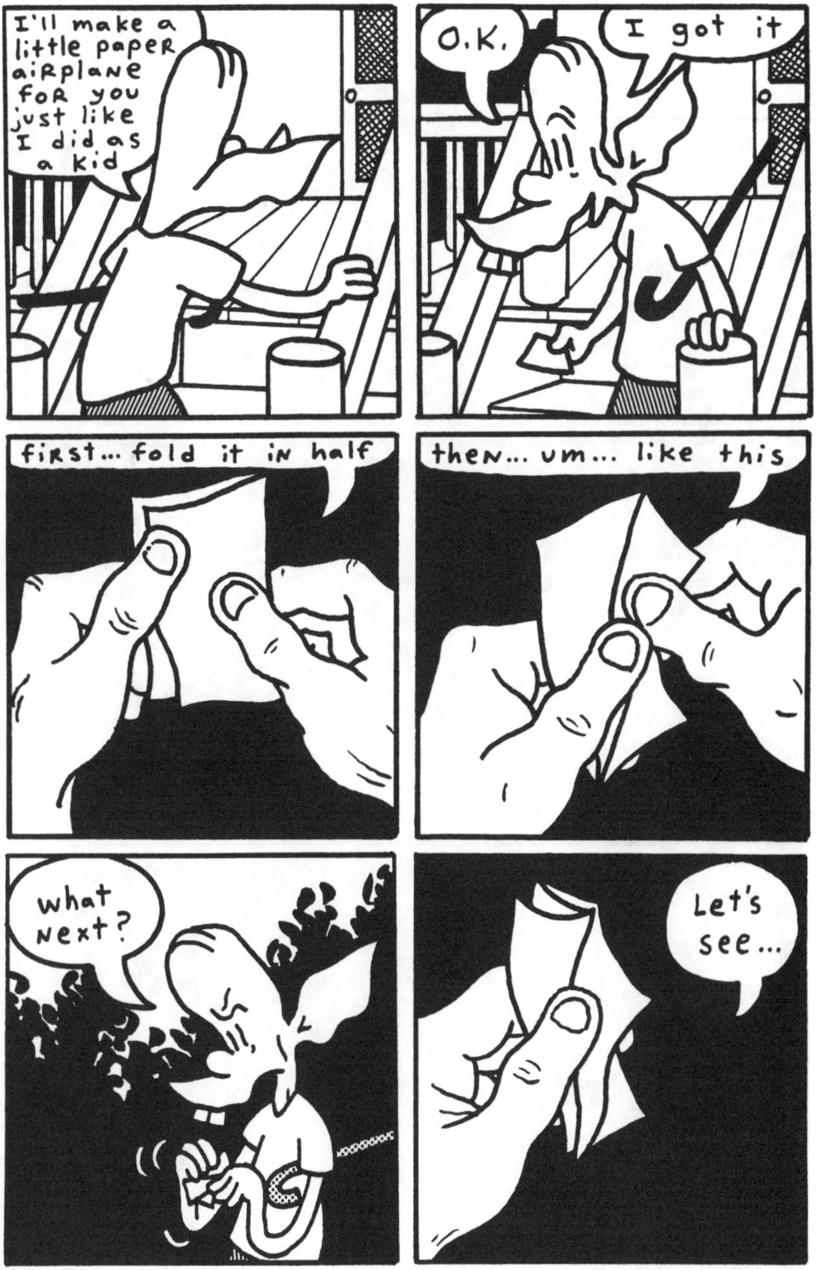
I'll make a little paper airplane for you just like I did as a kid
O.K.
I got it
first... fold it in half
then... um... like this
what next?
Let's see...

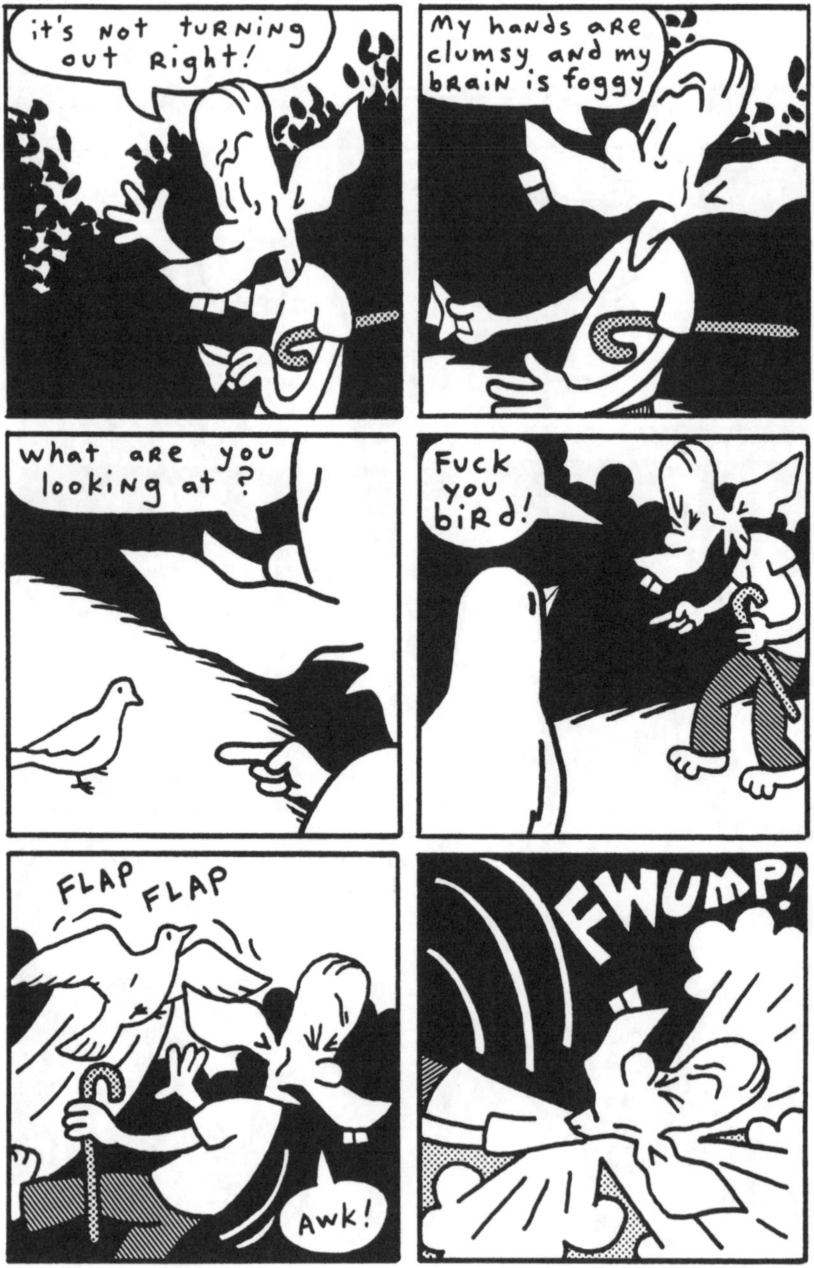
it's not turning out right!
My hands are clumsy and my brain is foggy
what are you looking at?
Fuck you bird!
FLAP FLAP
AWK!
FWUMP!

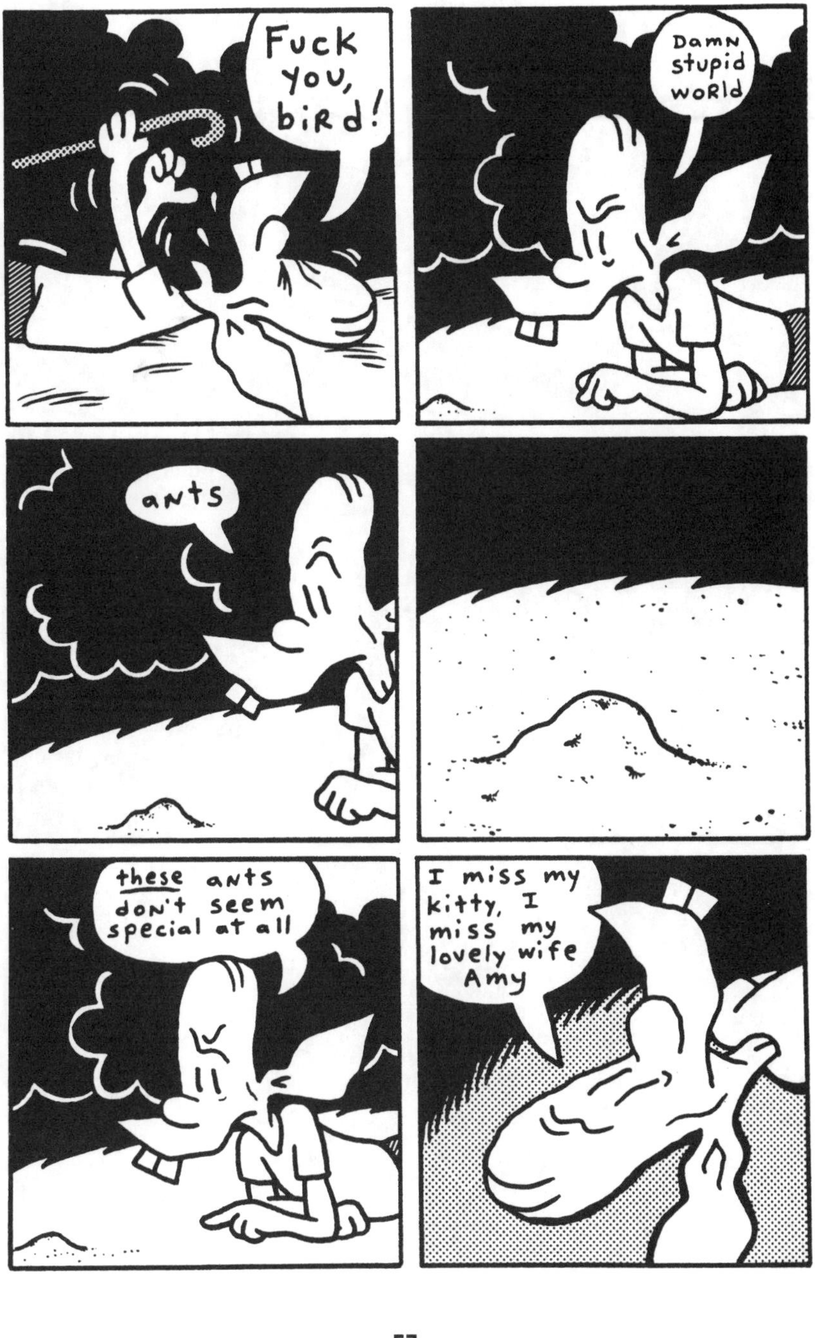
Fuck you, bird!
Damn stupid world
ants
these ants don't seem special at all
I miss my kitty, I miss my lovely wife Amy

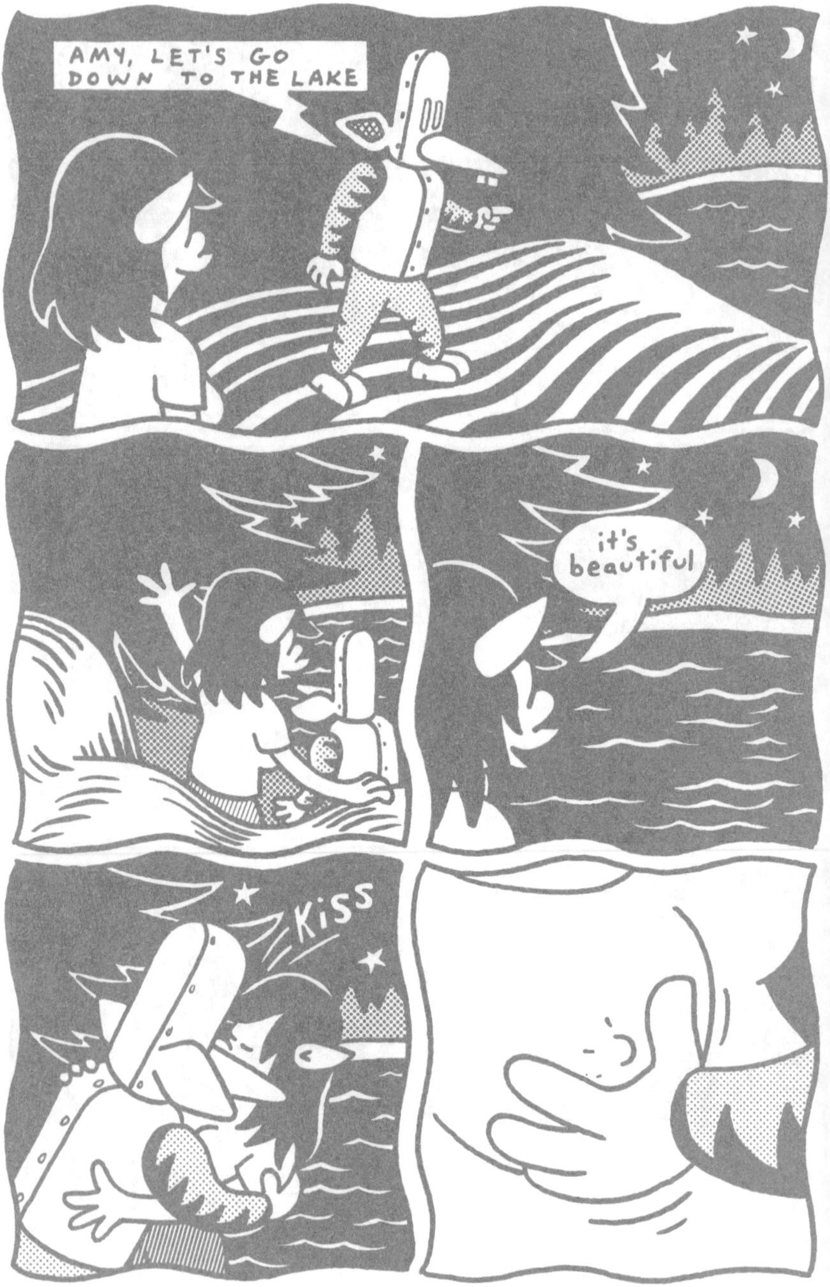
AMY, LET'S GO DOWN TO THE LAKE
it's beautiful
KiSS

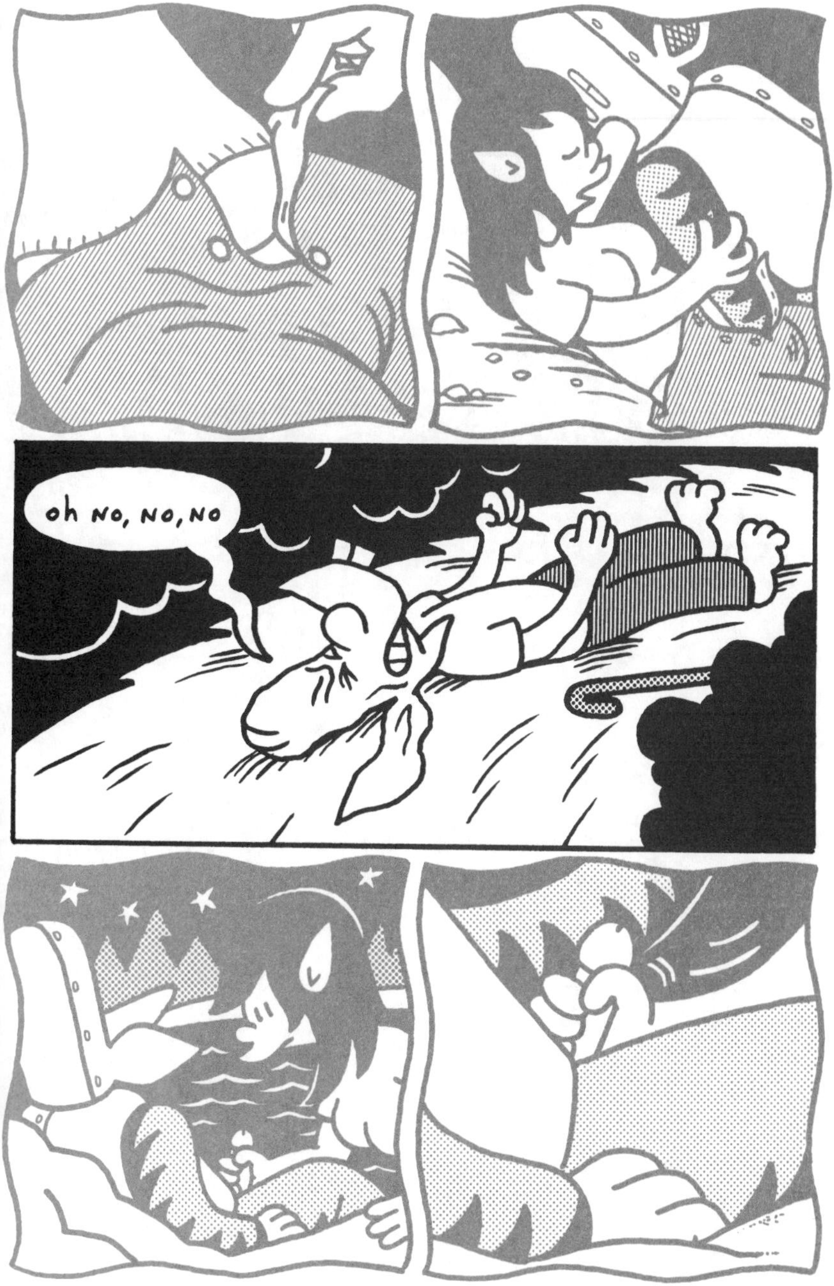
oh NO, NO, NO

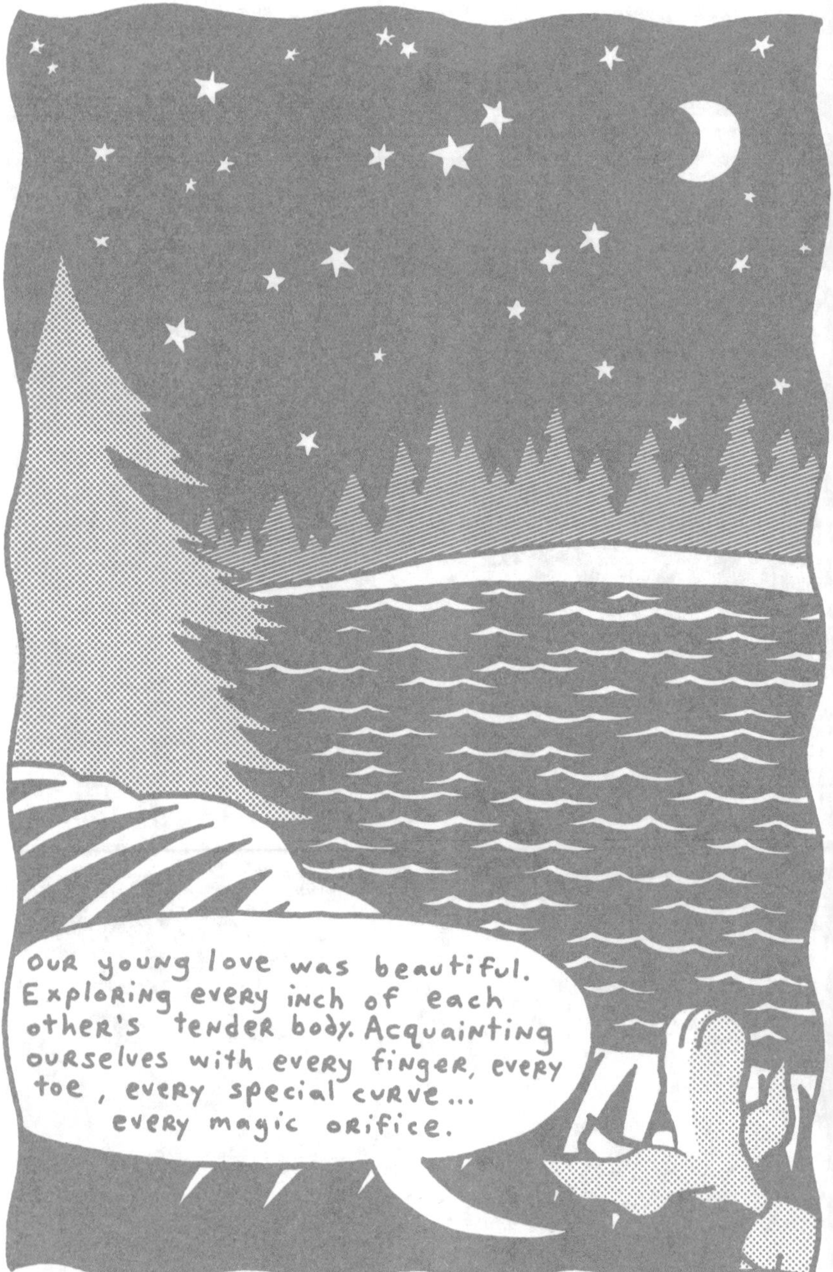
OUR young love was beautiful. Exploring every inch of each other's tender body. Acquainting ourselves with every finger, every toe, every special curve... every magic orifice.

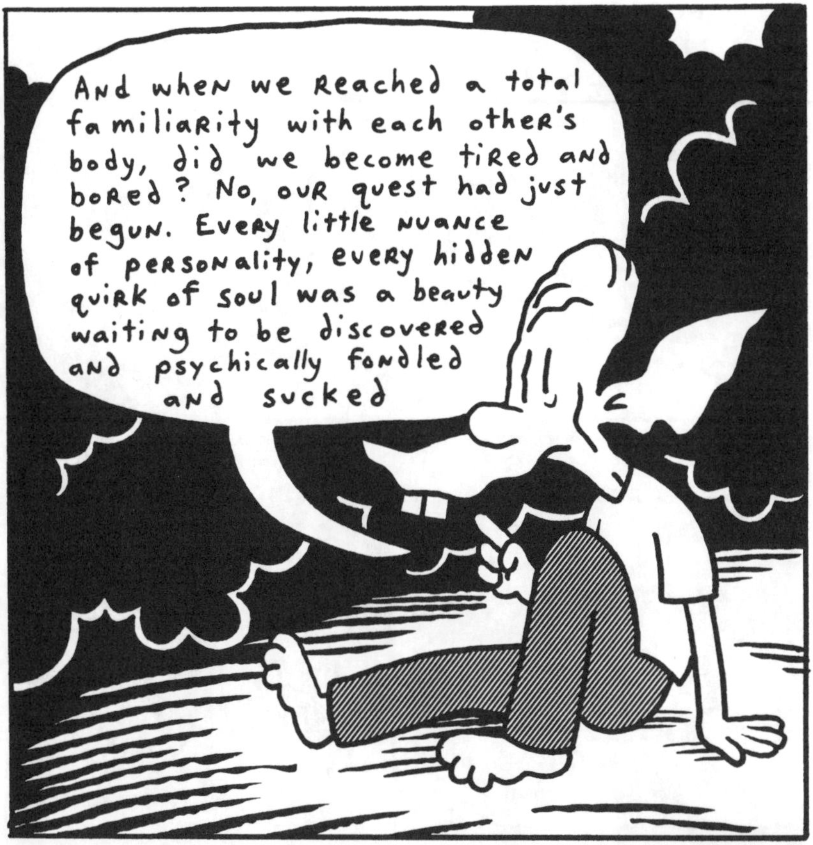
And when we reached a total familiarity with each other's body, did we become tired and bored? No, our quest had just begun. Every little nuance of personality, every hidden quirk of soul was a beauty waiting to be discovered and psychically fondled and sucked

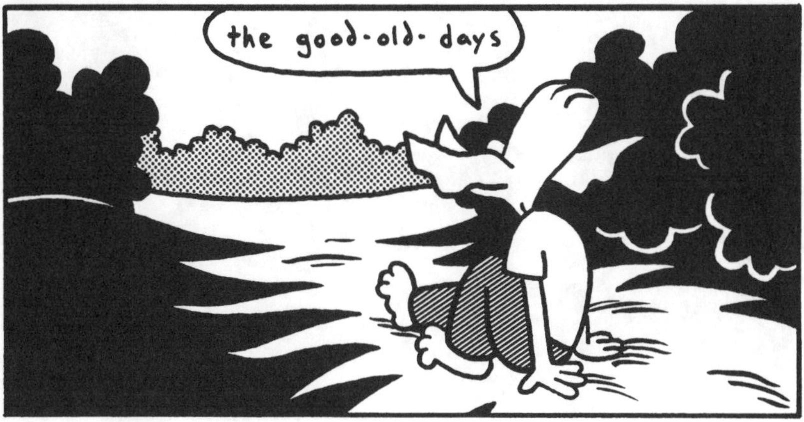
the good-old-days

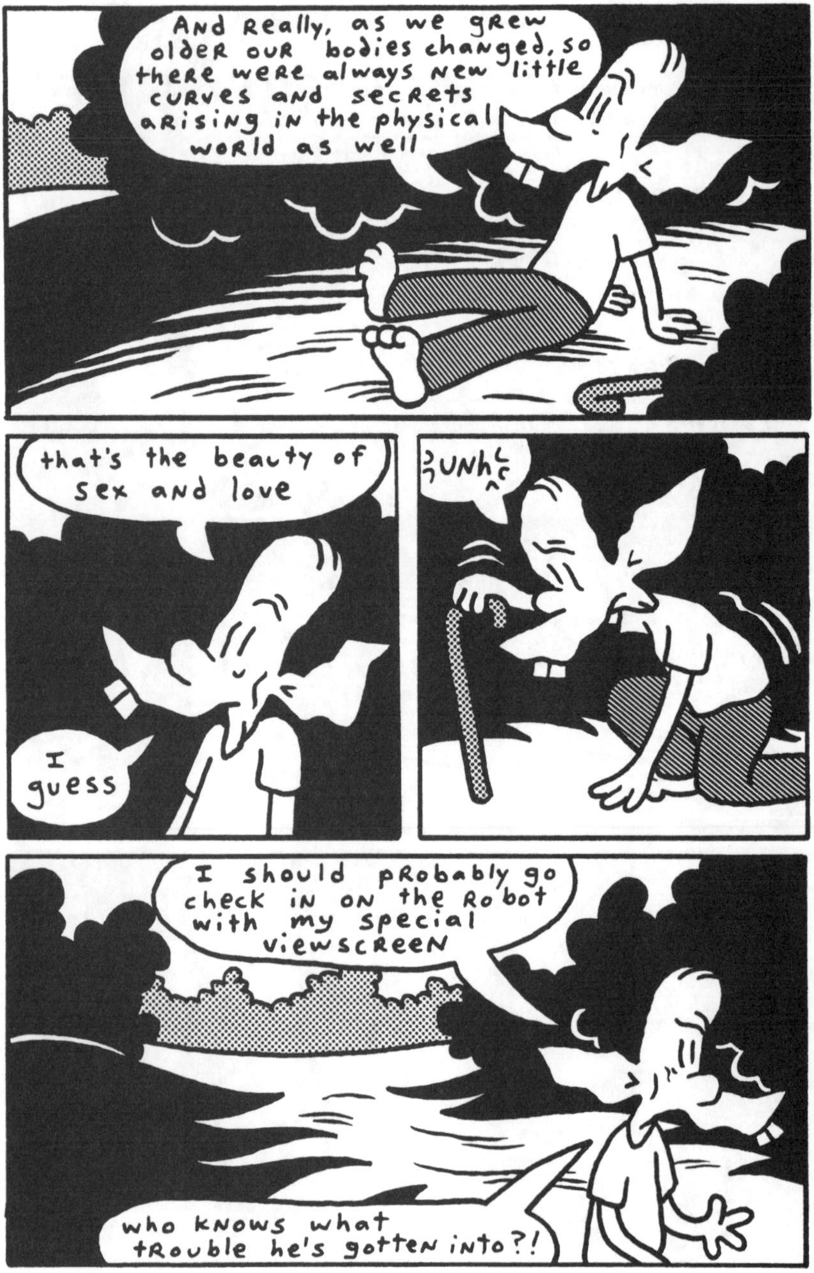
And really, as we grew older our bodies changed, so there were always new little curves and secrets arising in the physical world as well
that's the beauty of sex and love
I guess
UNh
I should probably go check in on the Robot with my special viewscreen
who knows what trouble he's gotten into?!

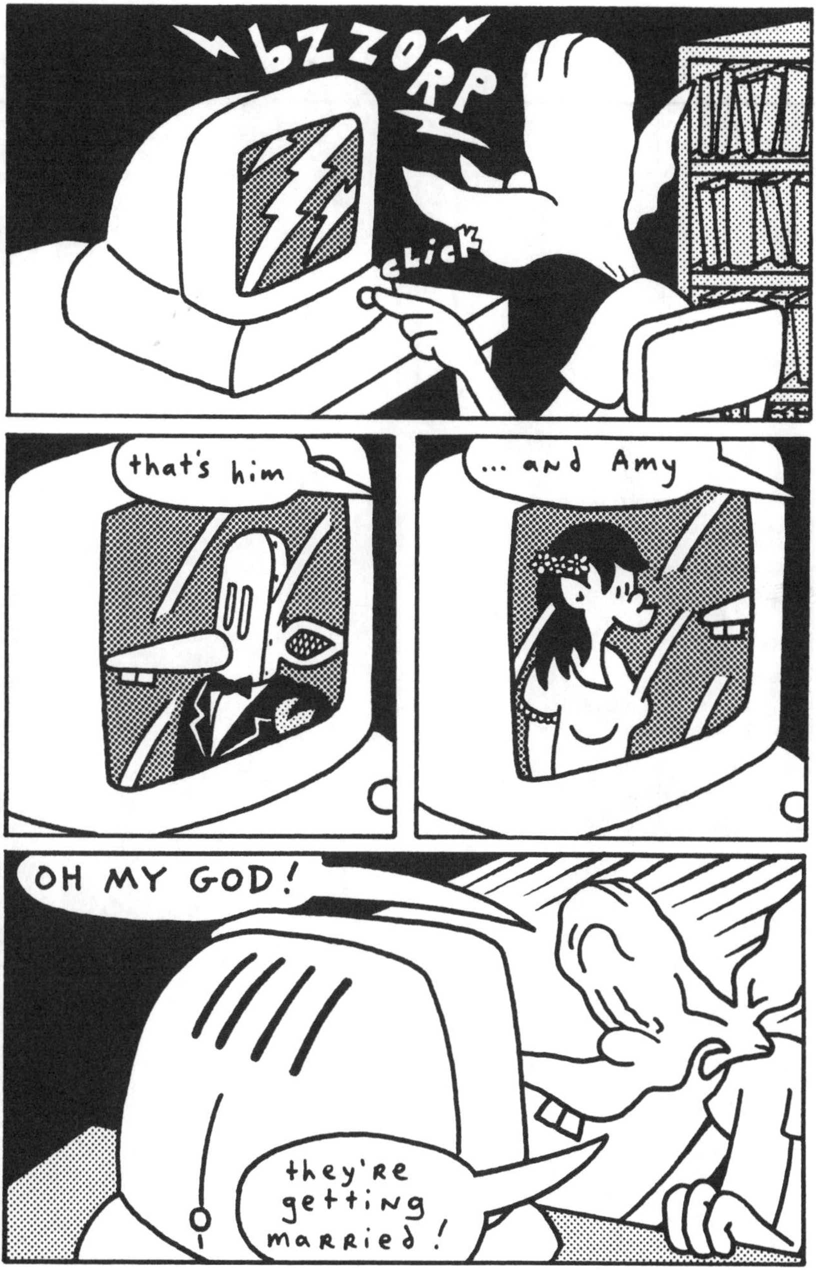
bzzorp
click
that's him
... and Amy
OH MY GOD!
they're getting married!

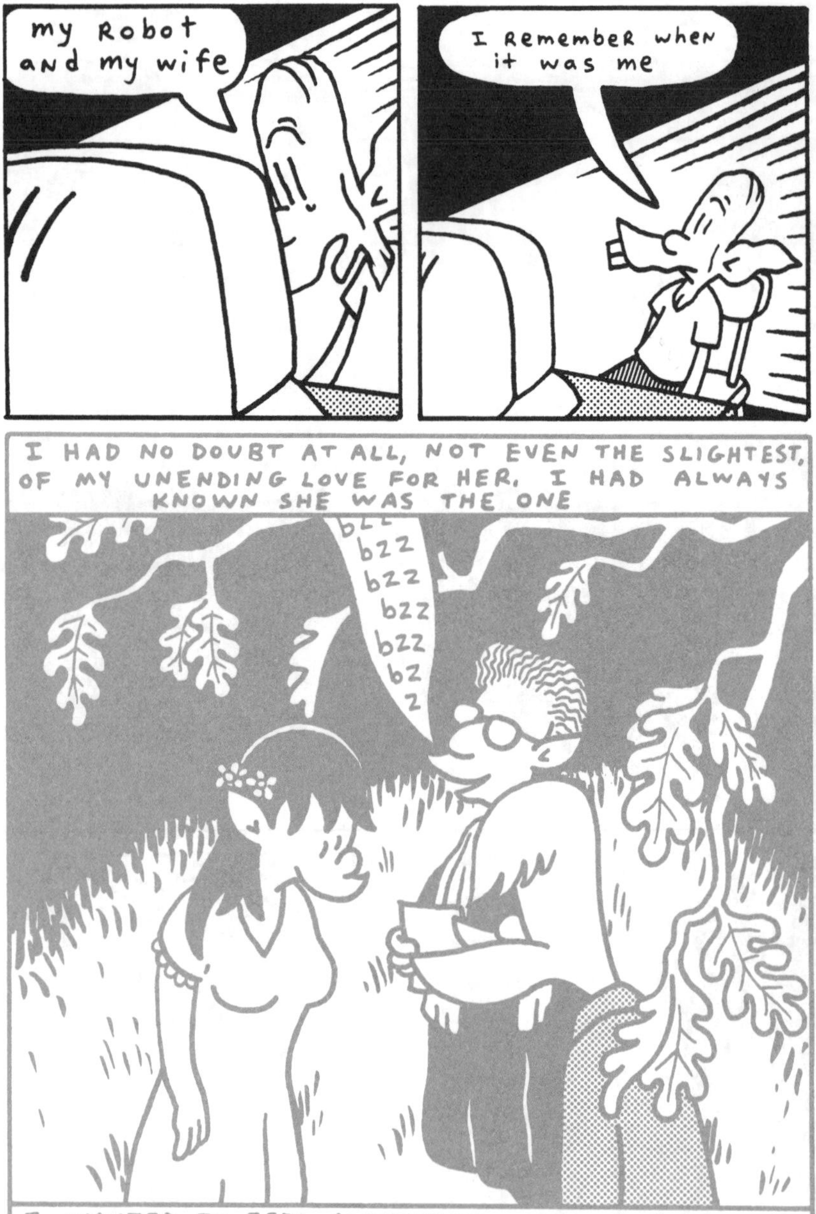
my Robot and my wife
I Remember when it was me
I HAD NO DOUBT AT ALL, NOT EVEN THE SLIGHTEST, OF MY UNENDING LOVE FOR HER. I HAD ALWAYS KNOWN SHE WAS THE ONE
bzz bzz bzz bzz bz z
I WANTED TO FEEL SOMETHING COSMIC DURING THE CEREMONY. THE MINISTER'S VOICE WAS A DISTANT BUZZING

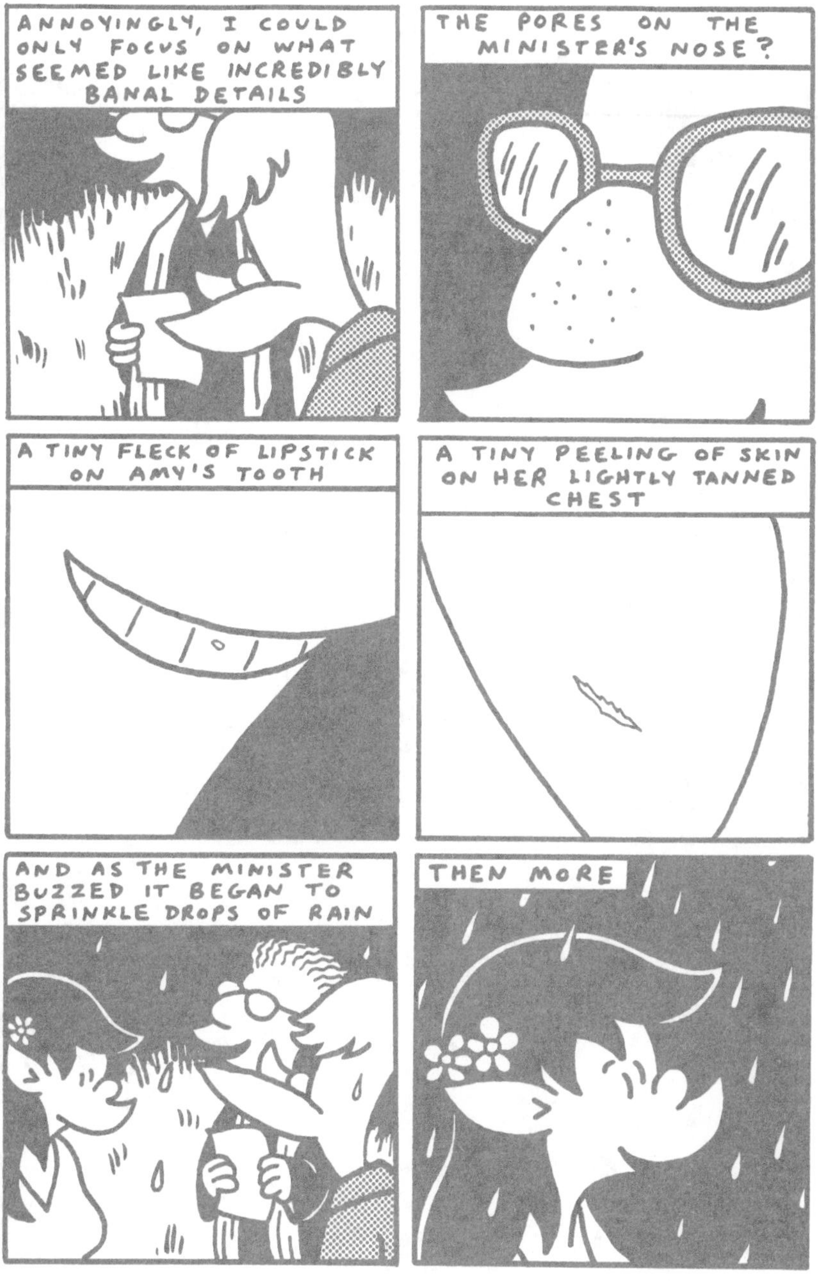
ANNOYINGLY, I COULD ONLY FOCUS ON WHAT SEEMED LIKE INCREDIBLY BANAL DETAILS
THE PORES ON THE MINISTER'S NOSE?
A TINY FLECK OF LIPSTICK ON AMY'S TOOTH
A TINY PEELING OF SKIN ON HER LIGHTLY TANNED CHEST
AND AS THE MINISTER BUZZED IT BEGAN TO SPRINKLE DROPS OF RAIN
THEN MORE

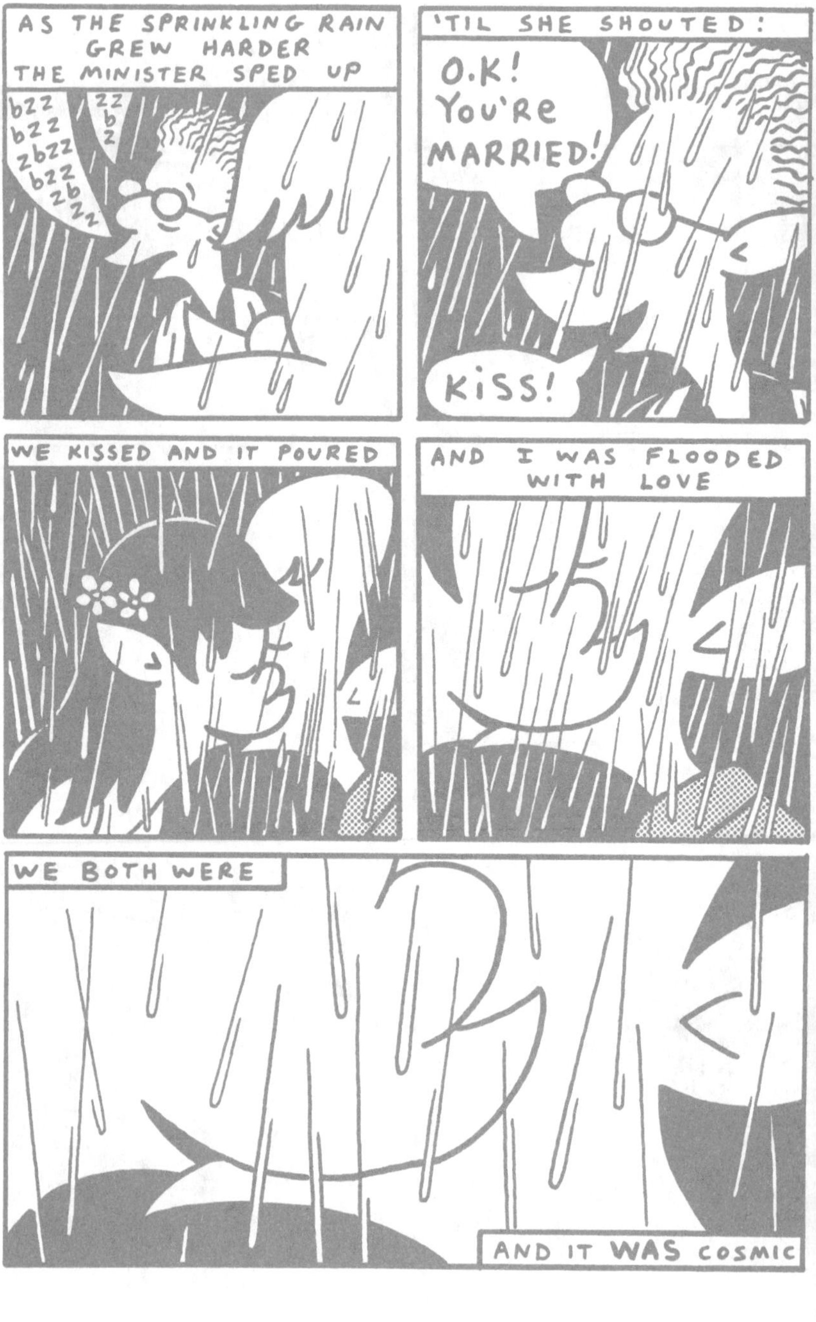
AS THE SPRINKLING RAIN GREW HARDER THE MINISTER SPED UP
bzz bzz zbzz bzz zb zz zz b z
'TIL SHE SHOUTED:
O.K! You're MARRIED!
KiSS!
WE KISSED AND IT POURED
AND I WAS FLOODED WITH LOVE
WE BOTH WERE
AND IT WAS COSMIC

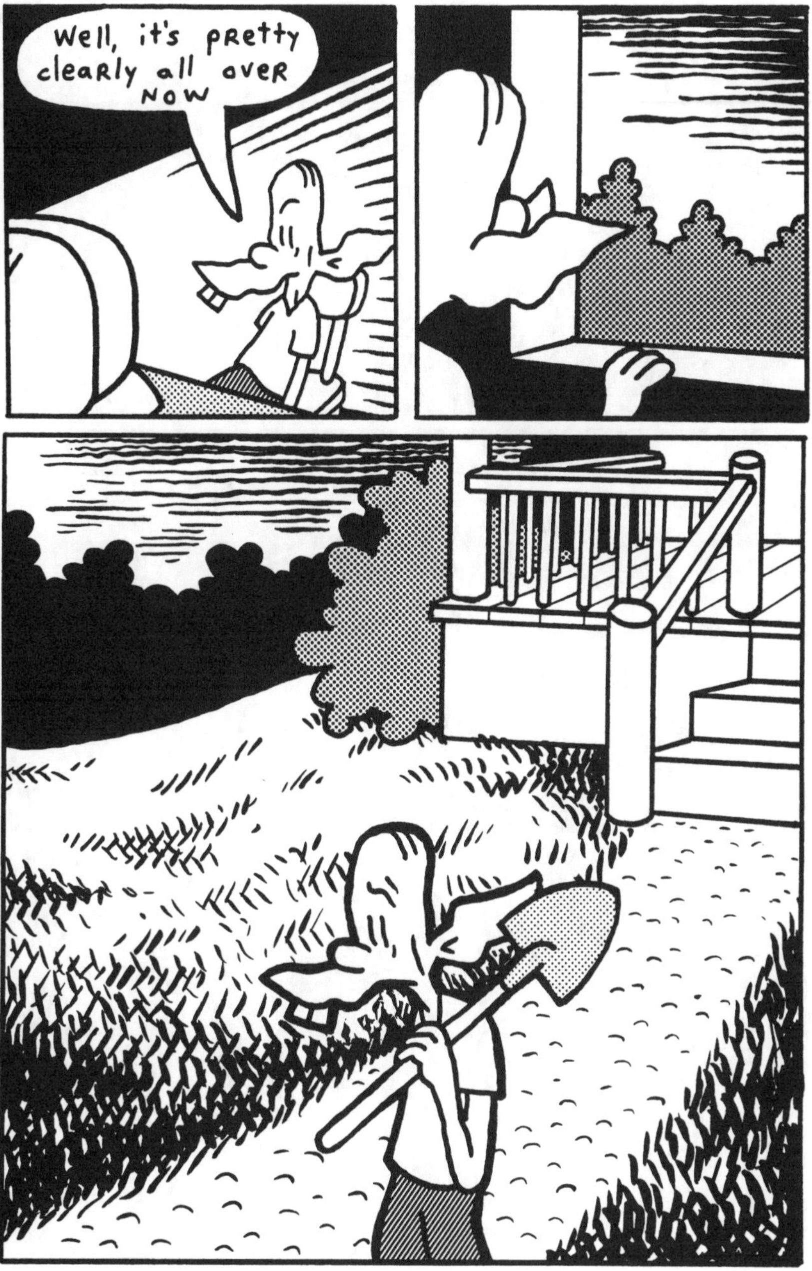
Well, it's pretty clearly all over NOW

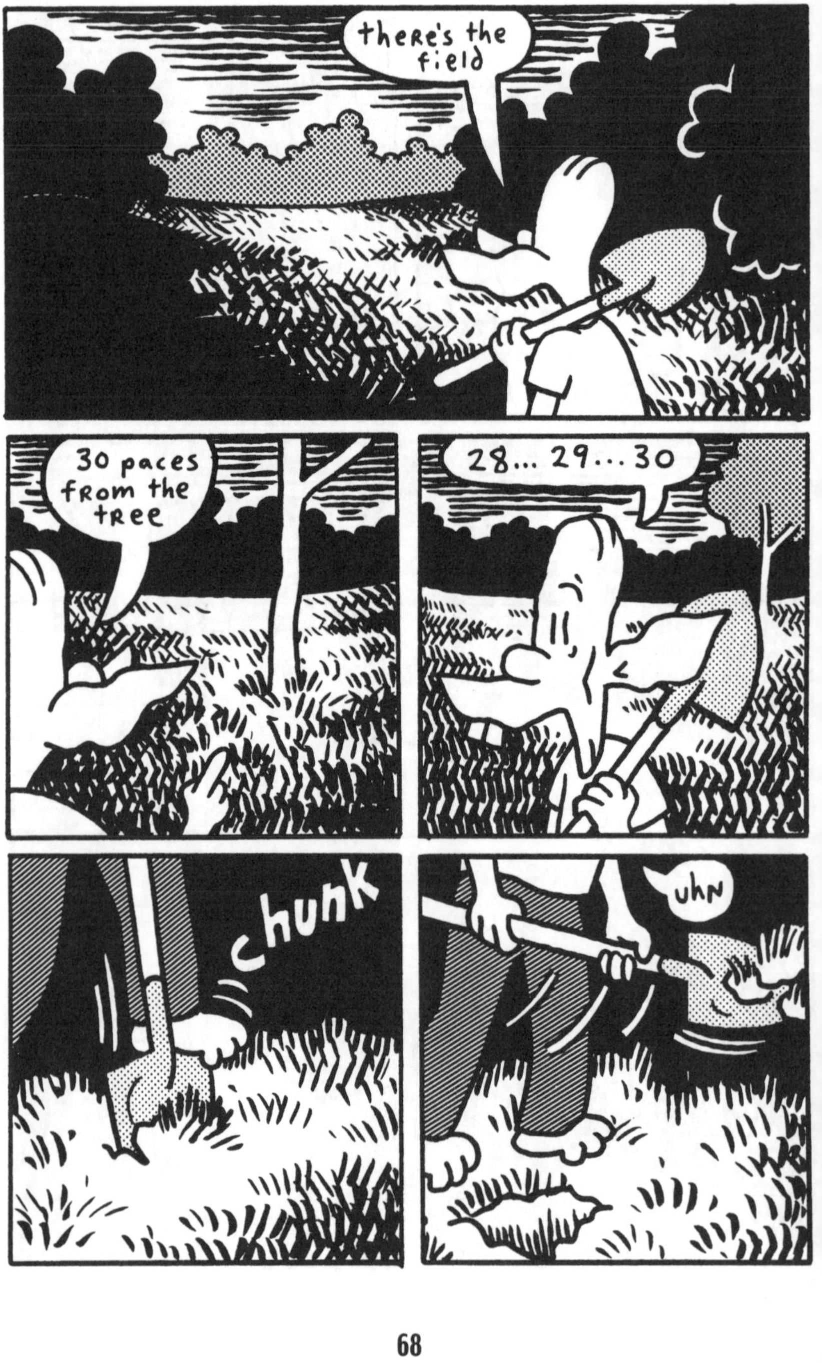
there's the field
30 paces from the tree
28... 29... 30
chunk
uhn

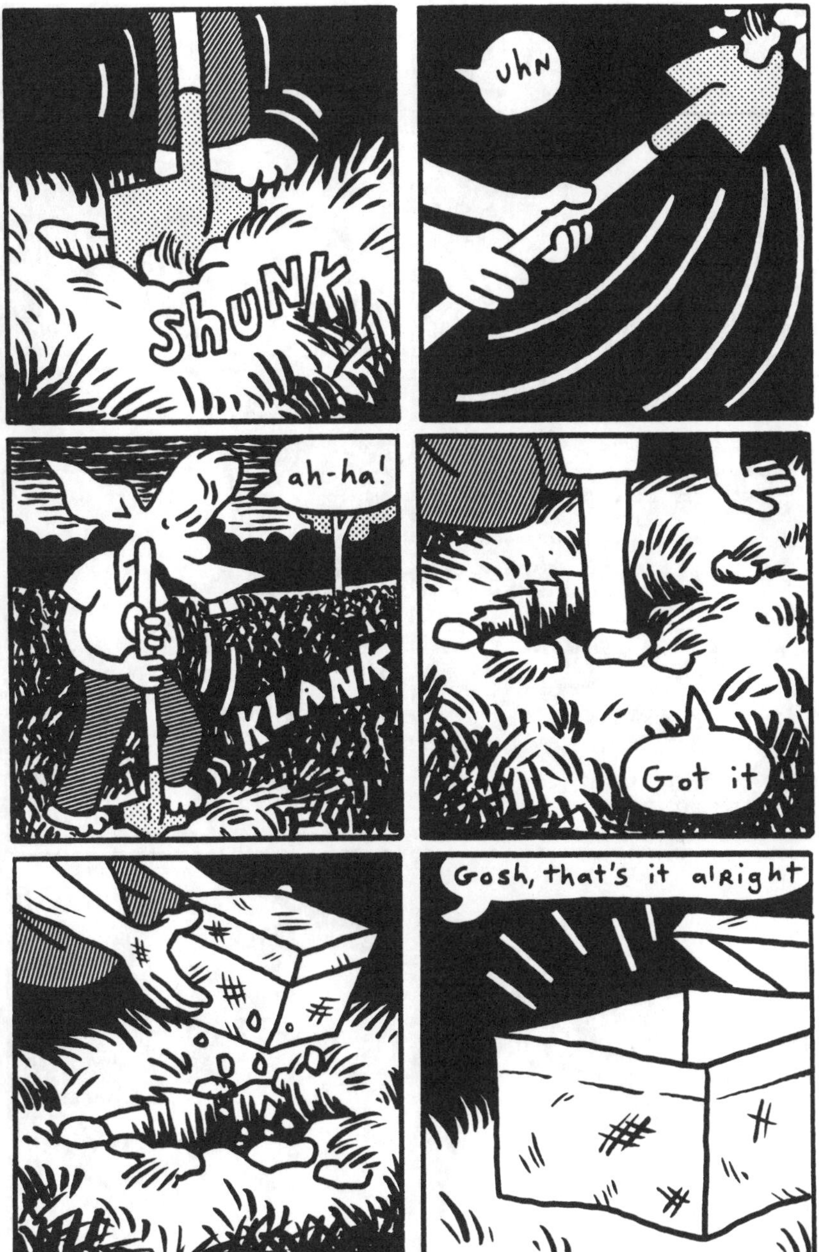
SHUNK
uhn
ah-ha!
KLANK
Got it
Gosh, that's it alright

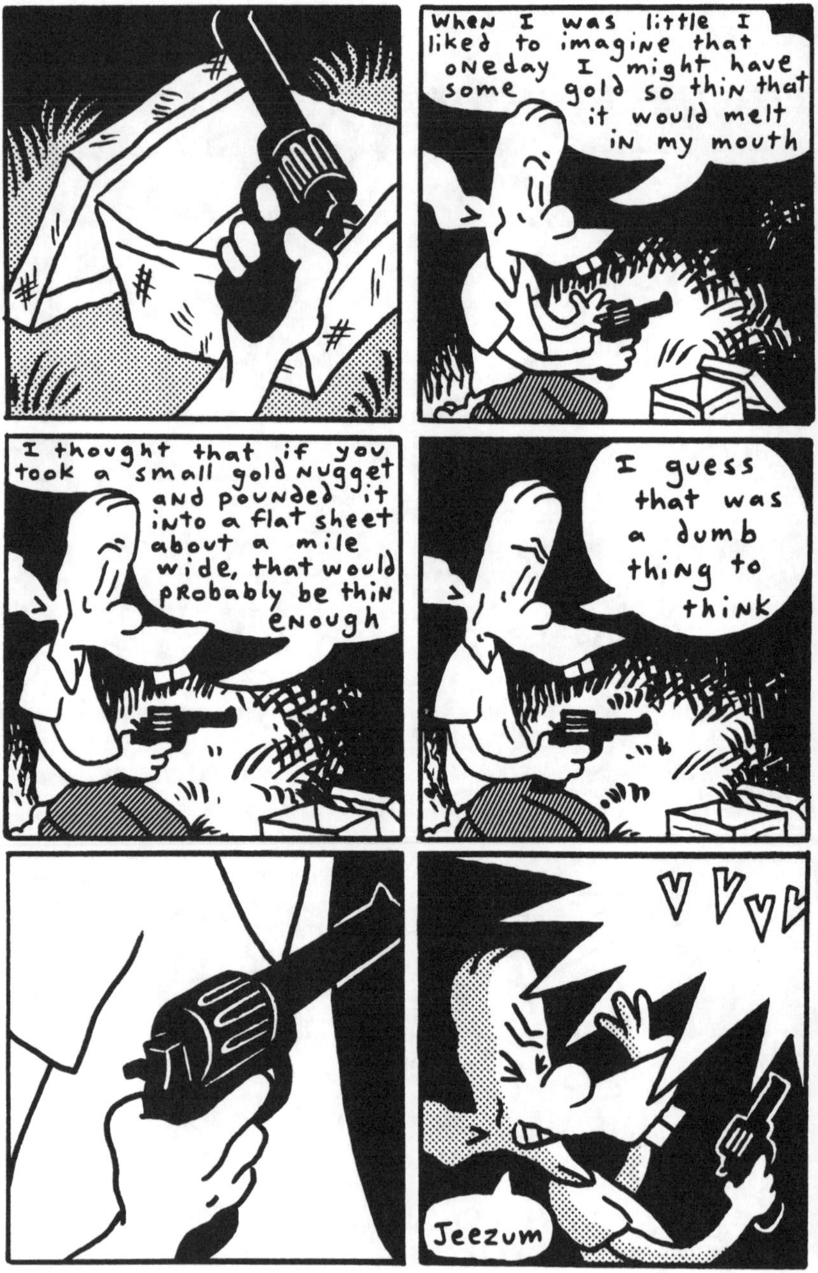
When I was little I liked to imagine that oneday I might have some gold so thin that it would melt in my mouth
I thought that if you took a small gold nugget and pounded it into a flat sheet about a mile wide, that would probably be thin enough
I guess that was a dumb thing to think
Jeezum

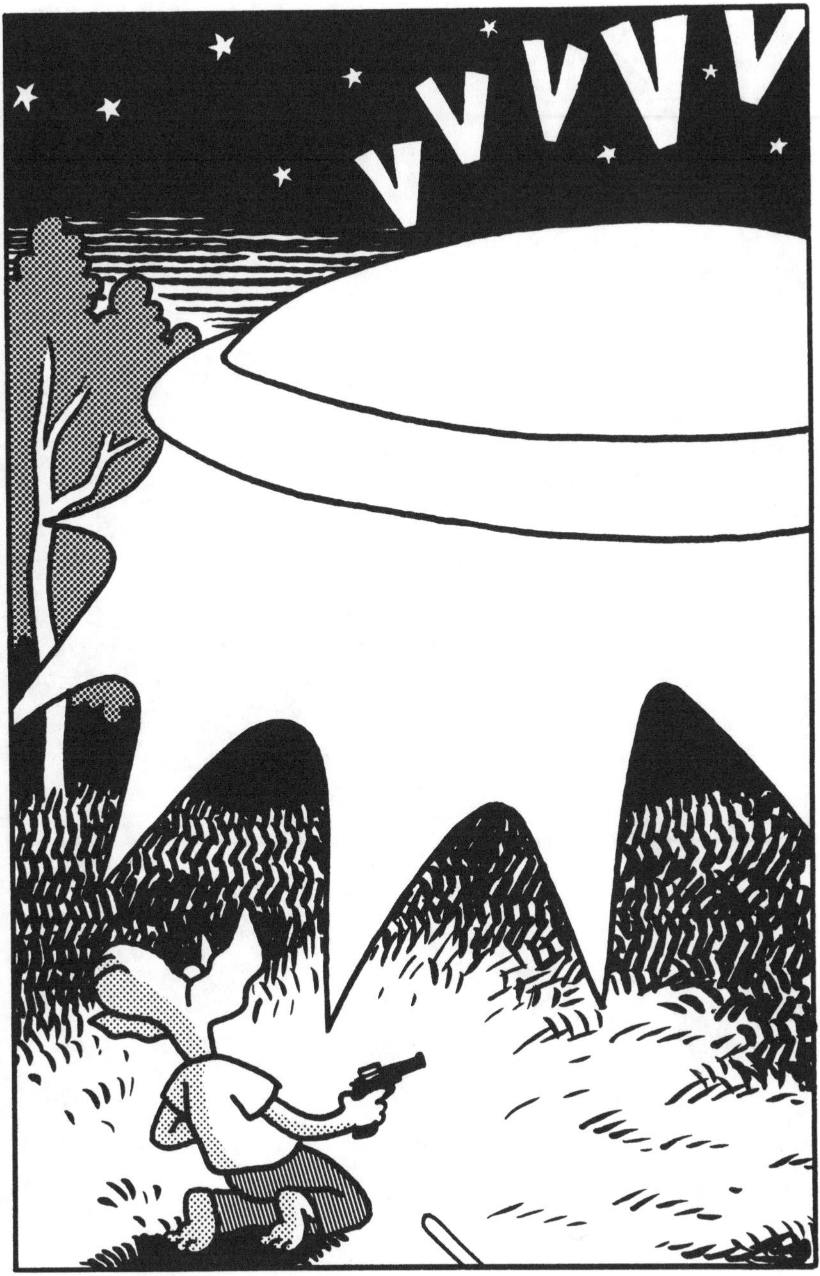
VVVVV

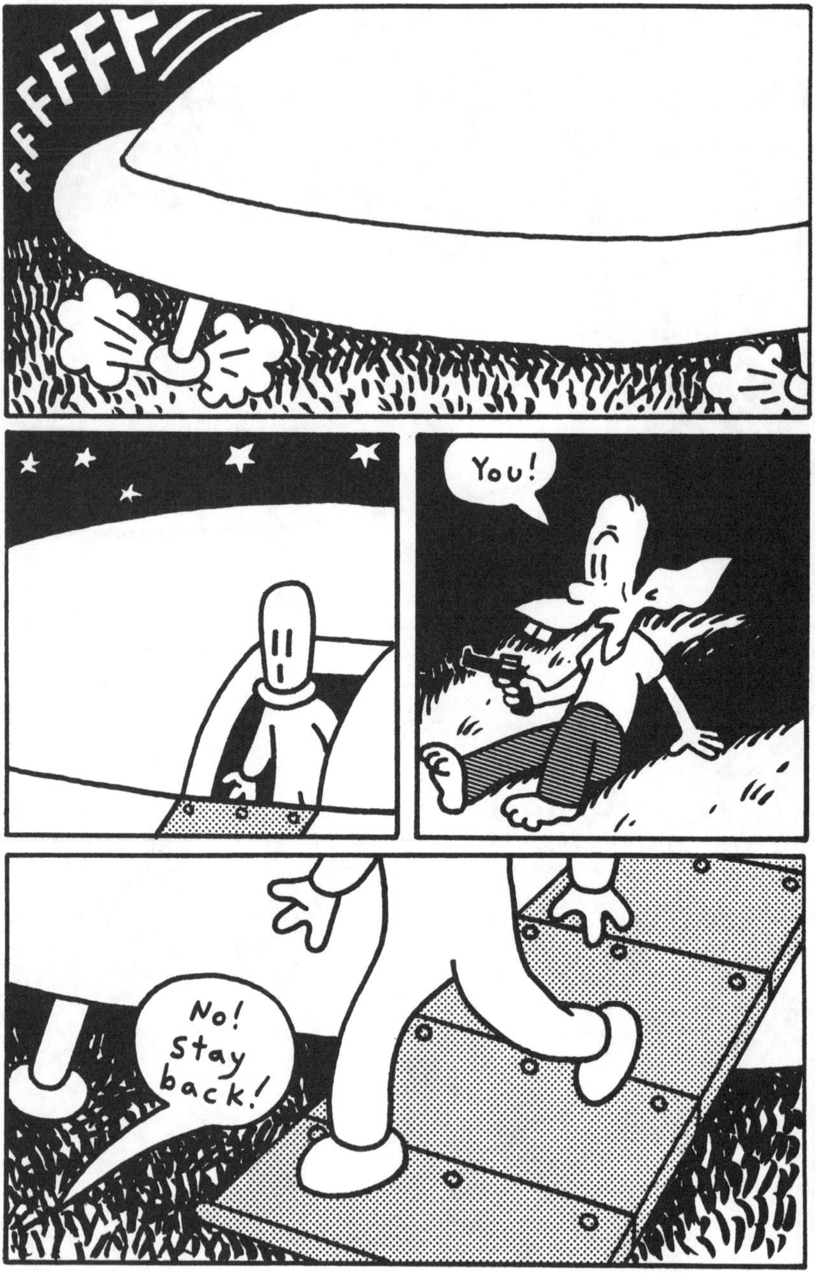
FFFFK
You!
No! Stay back!

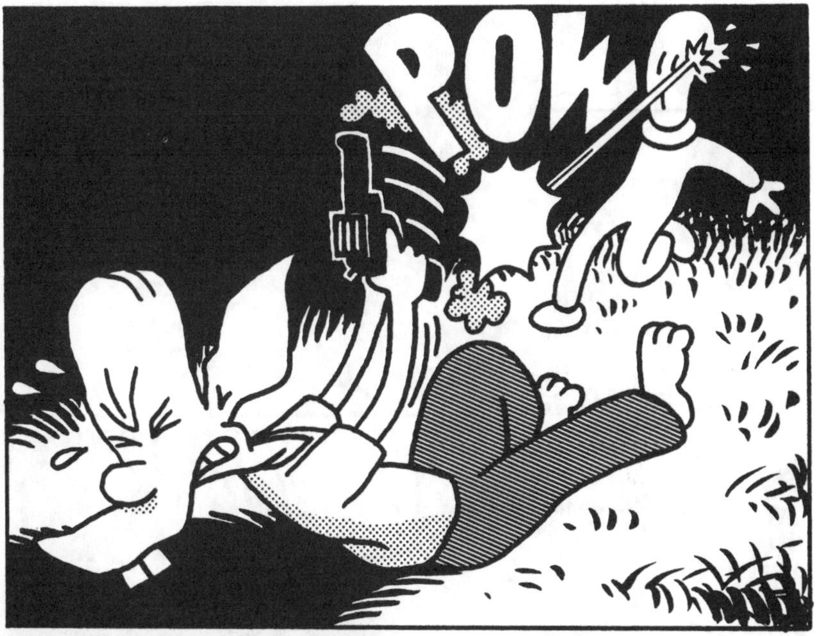
POW

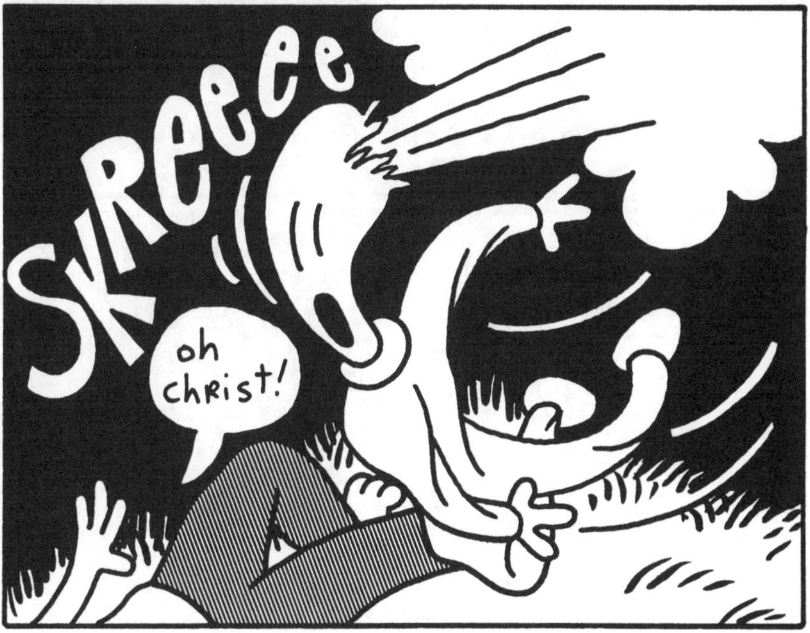
SKReeee
oh christ!

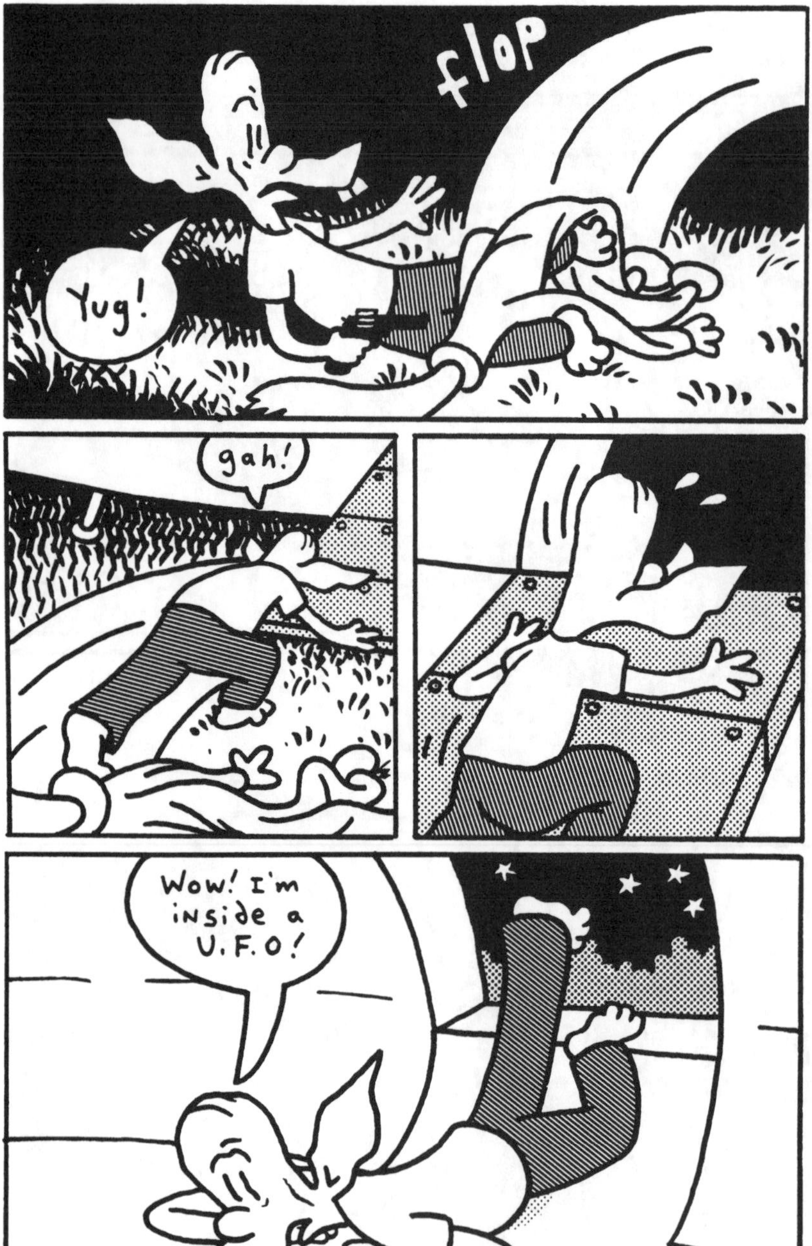
flop
Yug!
gah!
Wow! I'm inside a U.F.O!

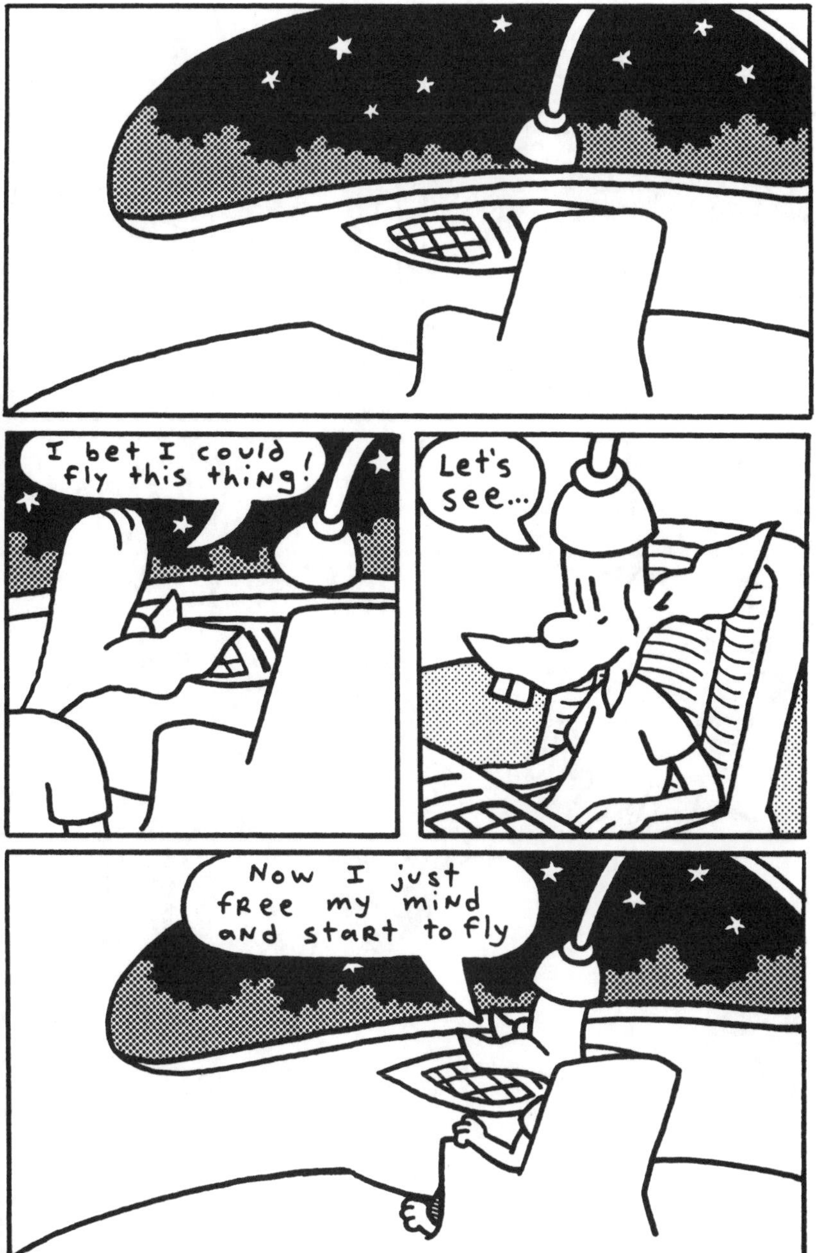
I bet I could fly this thing!
Let's see...
Now I just free my mind and start to fly

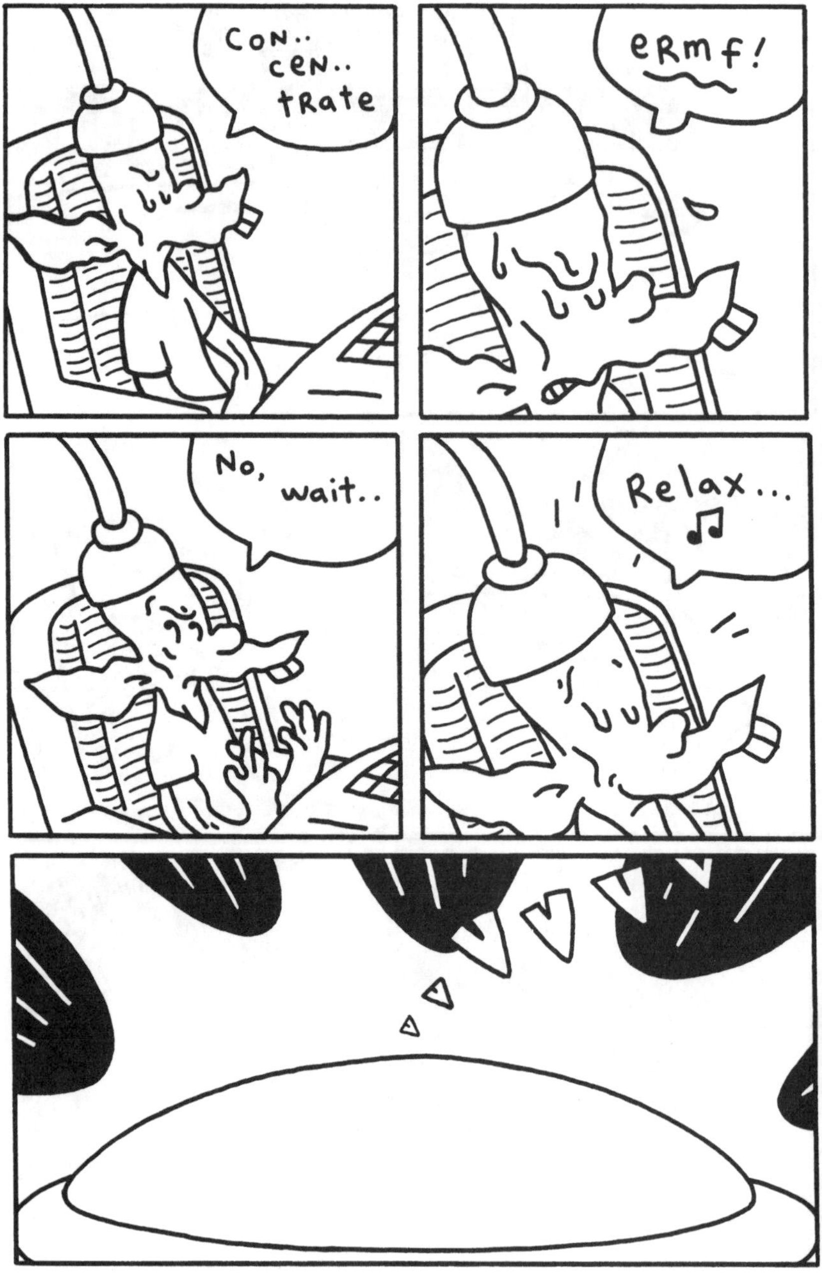
CON..
CeN..
tRate
eRmf!
No,
wait..
Relax...

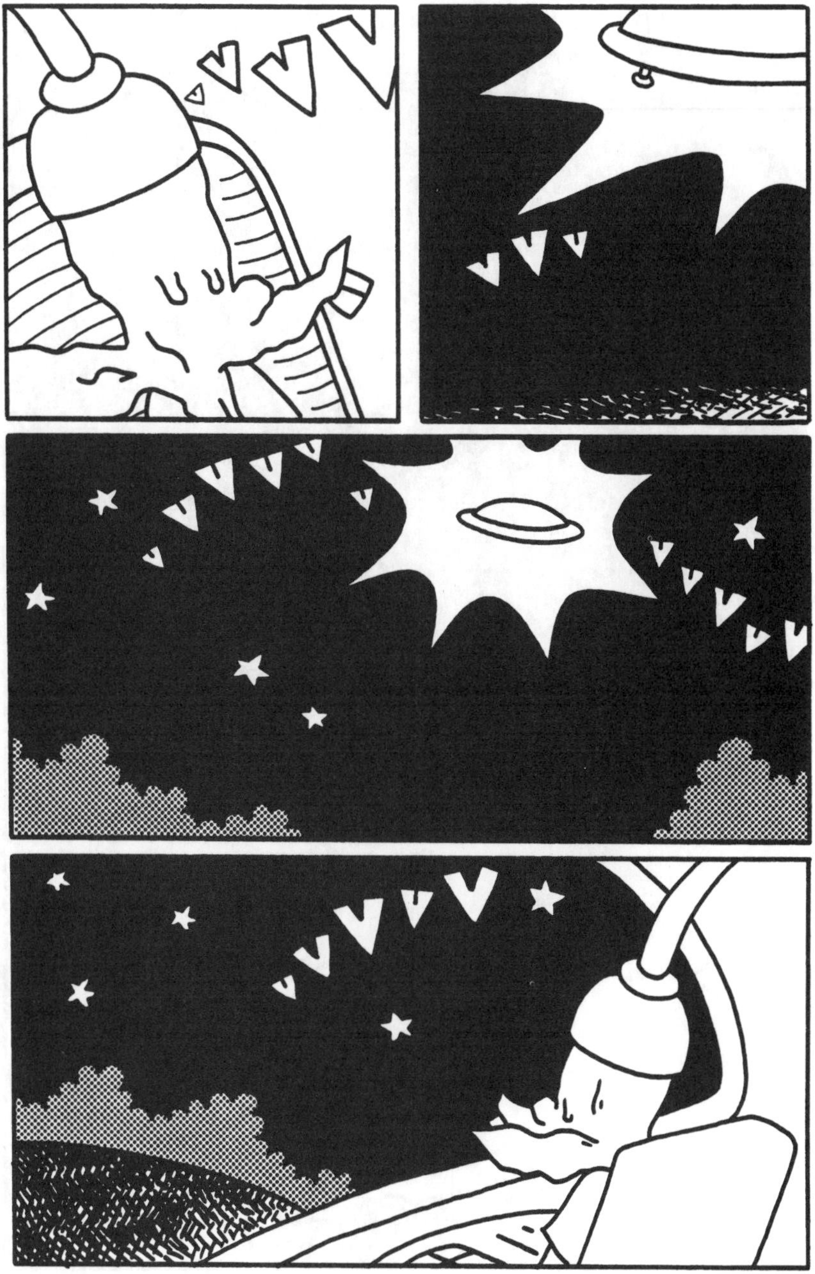

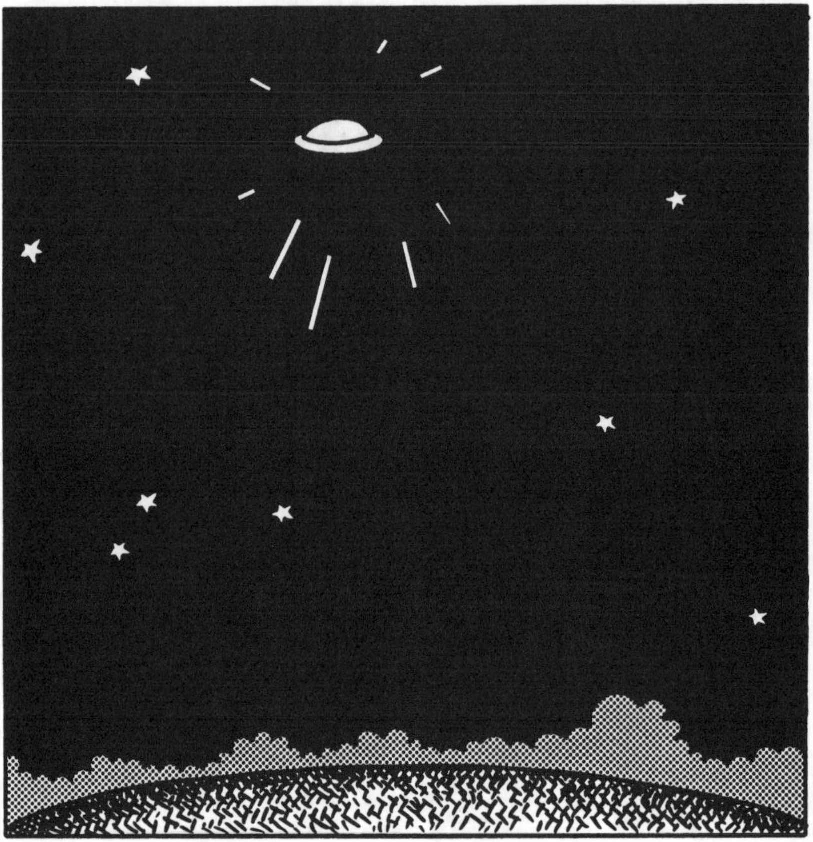

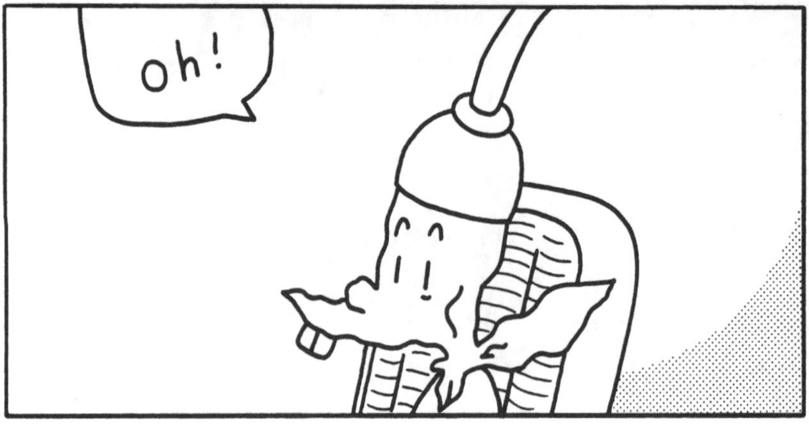
Oh!

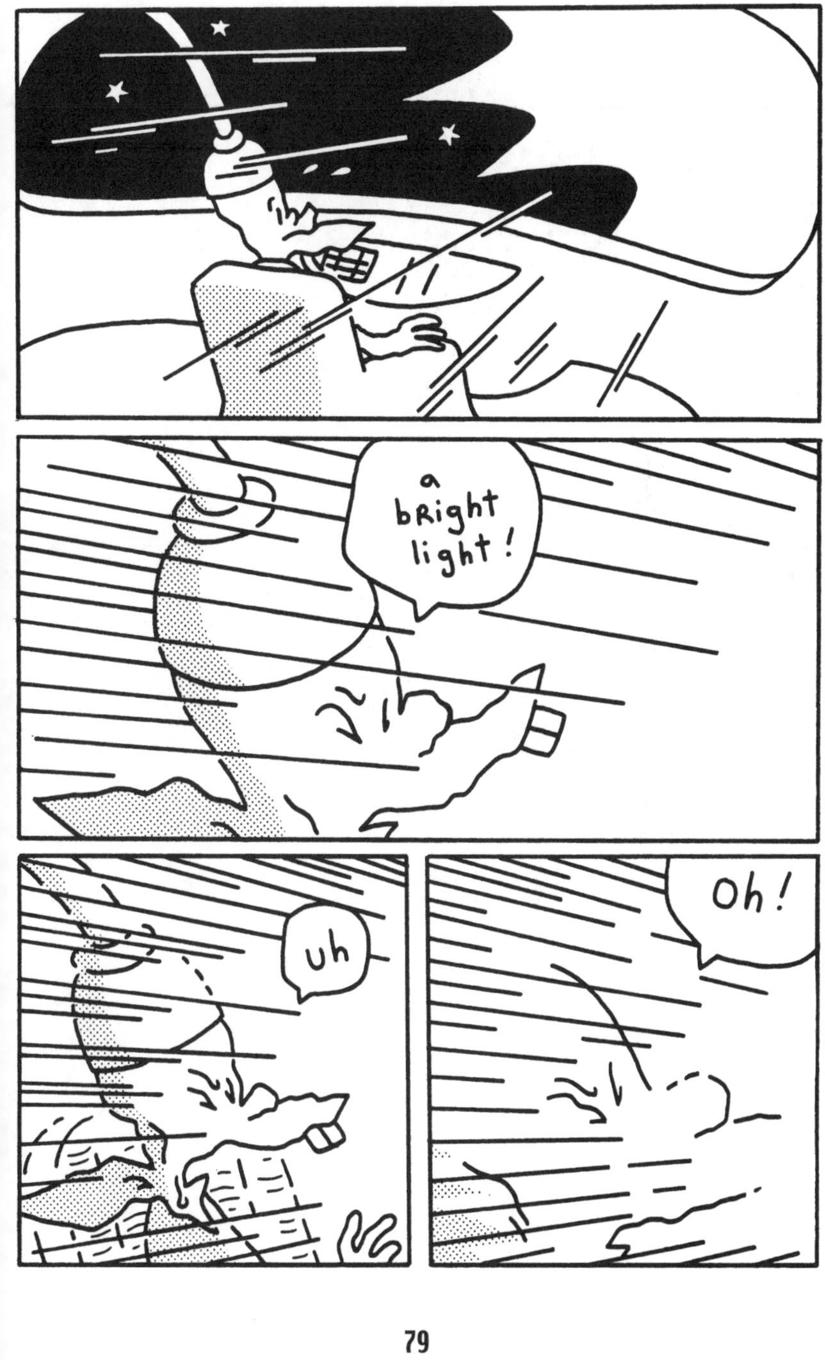
a bRight light!
uh
Oh!

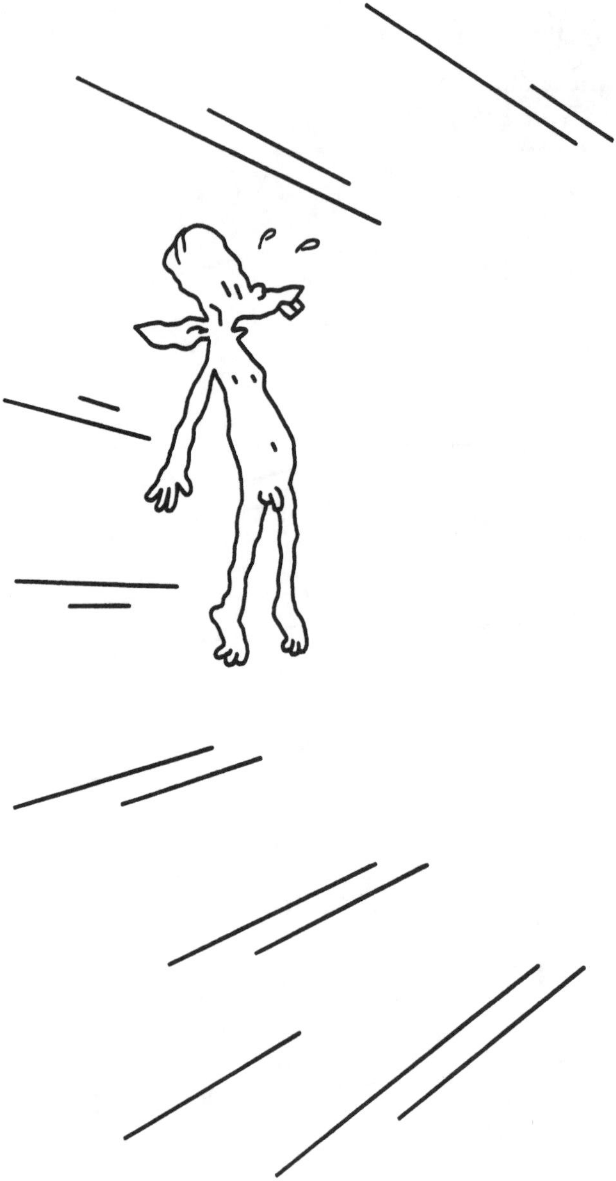

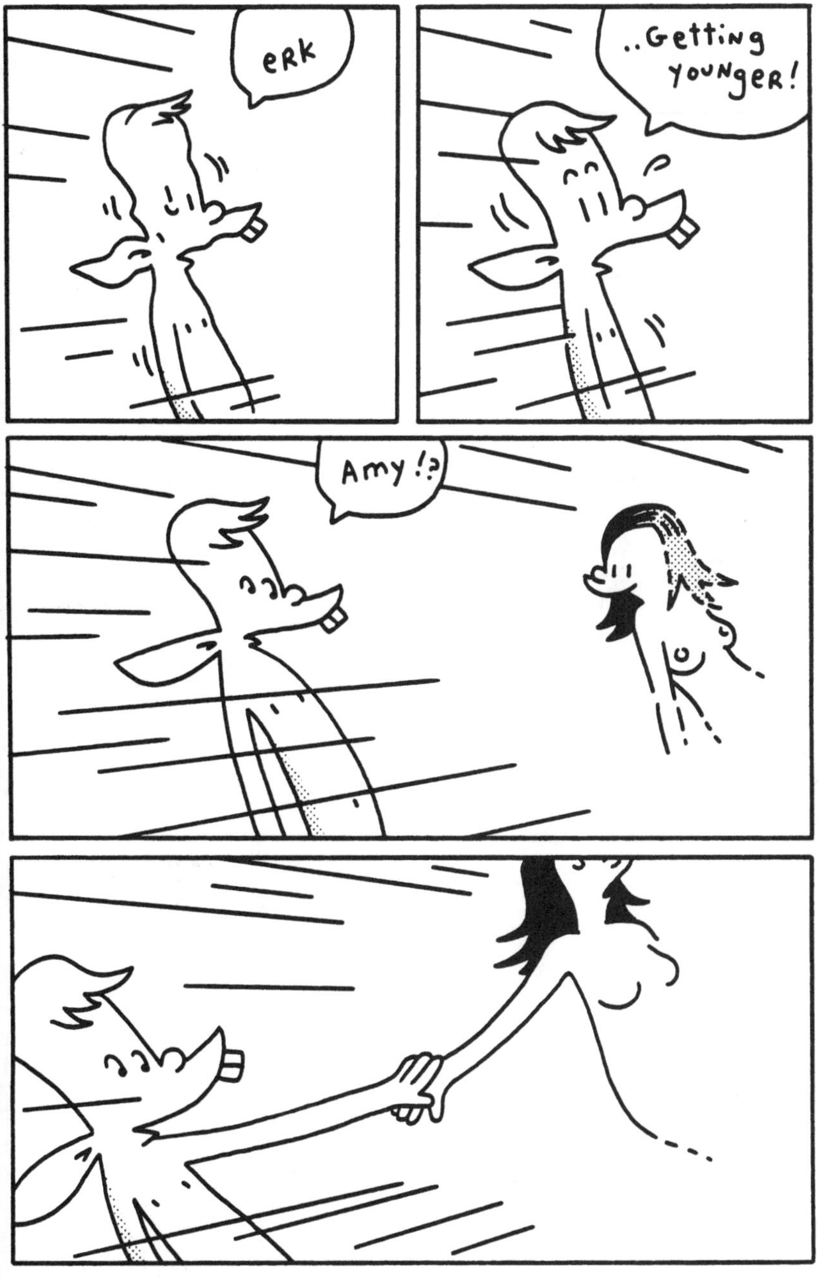
erk
..Getting younger!
Amy!?

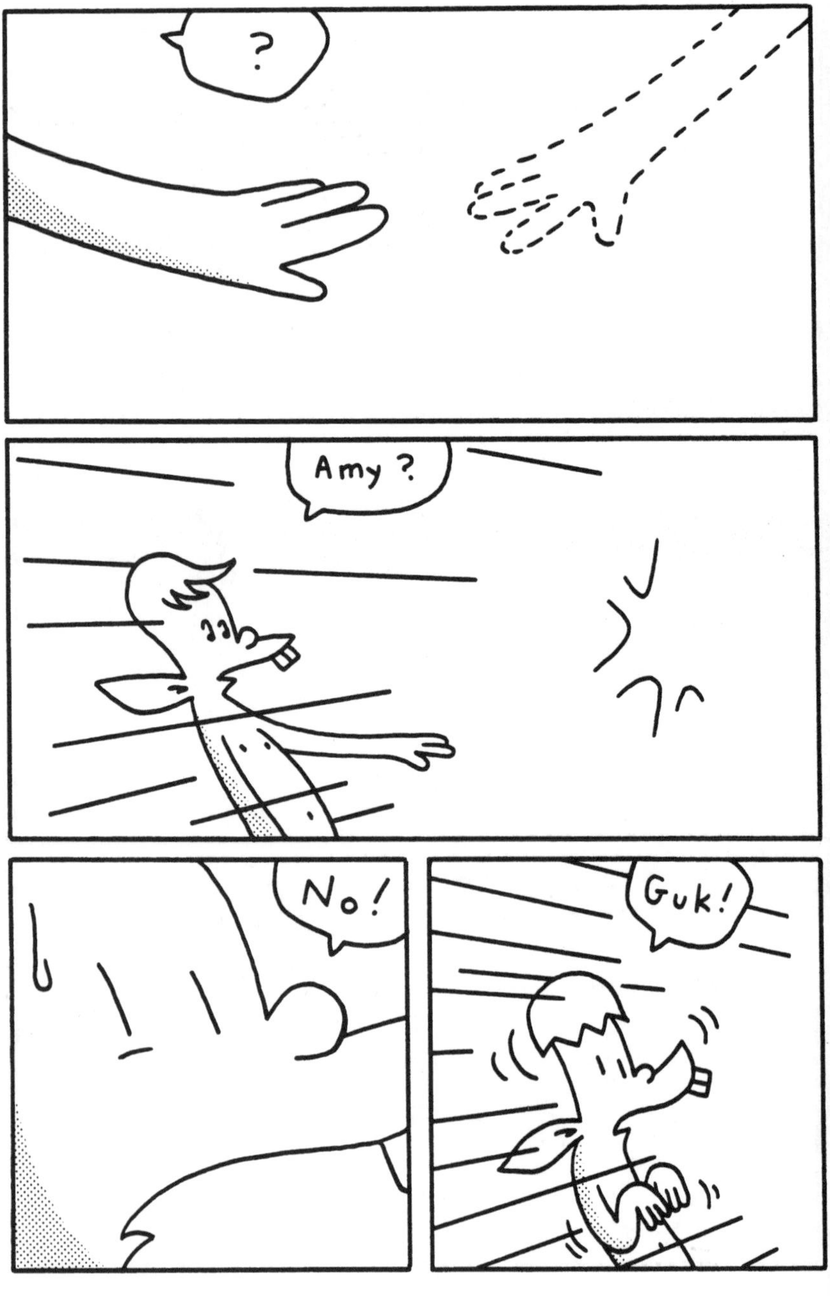
?
Amy?
No!
Guk!

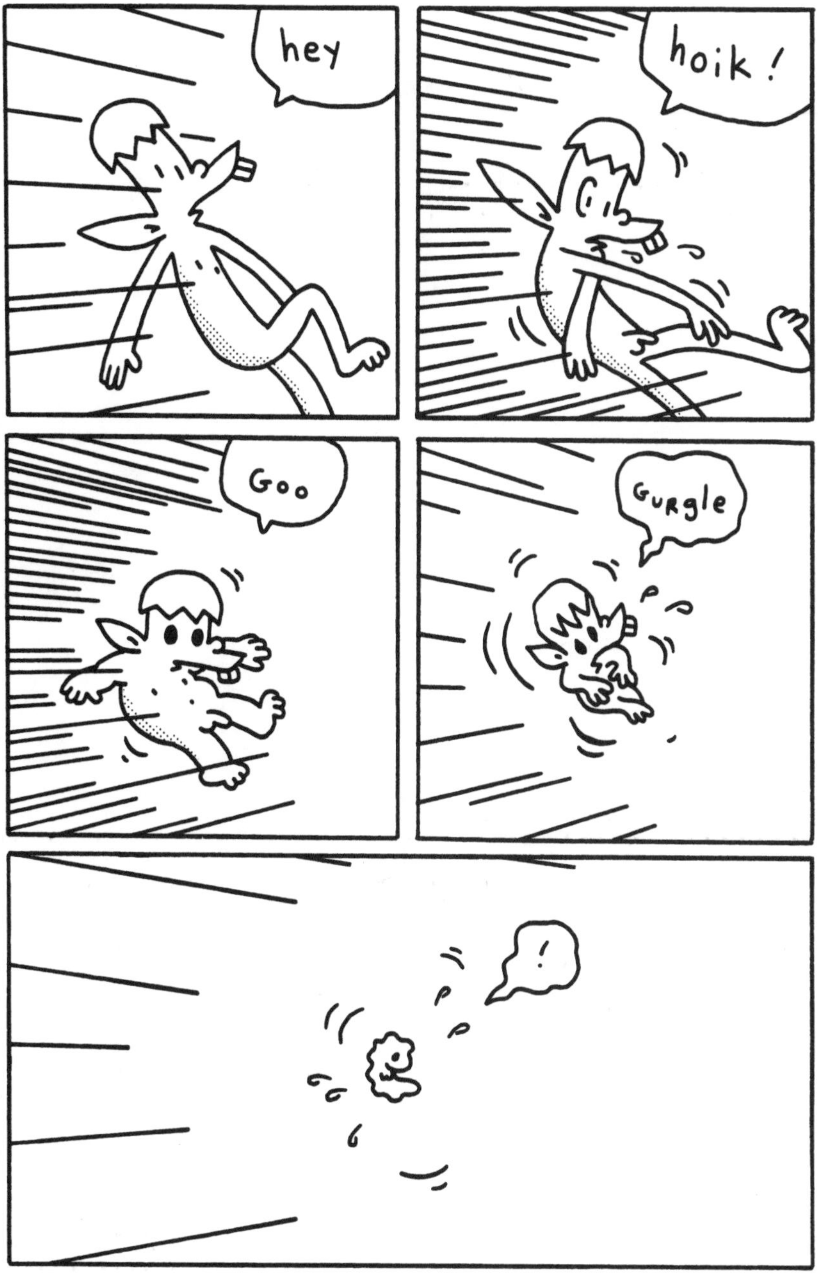
hey
hoik!
Goo
Gurgle
!

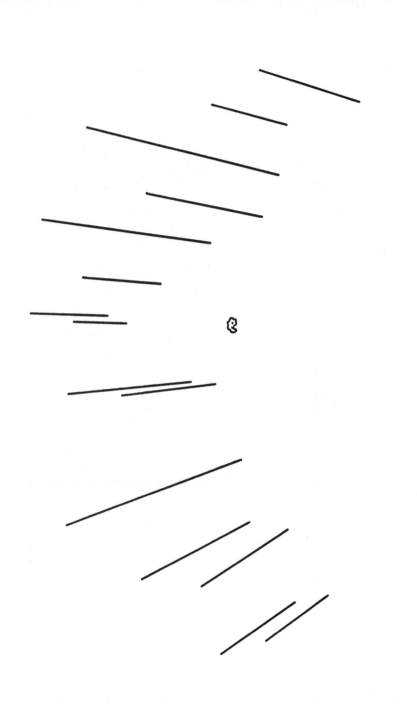

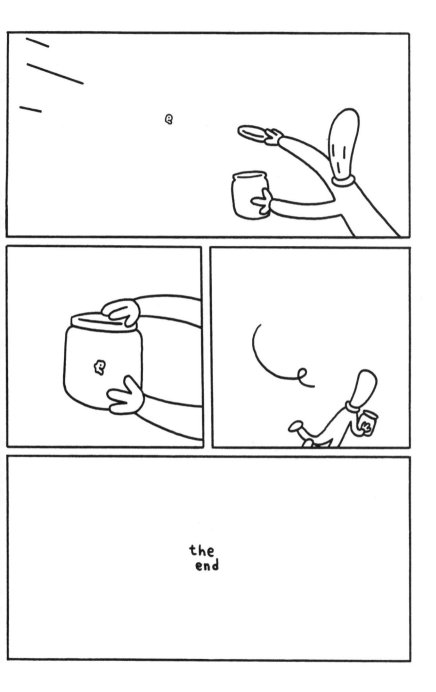

the
end